" Marketing is merely a civilized form of warfare in which most battles are won with words, ideas and disciplined thinking "

- Albert W. Emery: Noted US Advertising Executive

In loving memory of my sister Julie

MARKETING PLAN BUILDER
First edition

A practical guide to driving your business to reach its true potential

> ❝ Overnight miracles do not happen in marketing. You have to have the right product or service; you have to communicate the right message to the right people at the right time and the right place and you have to do it over and over again. Do this in a systematic manner and the results will follow. ❞   The author

GARTH KESTER

© 2018 KESTER MARKETING
All rights reserved. No part of this book may be reproduced or used in any manner without the express written permission of the publisher except for the use of brief quotations in a book review.
ISBN: 9781980287711

http://www.marketingplanbuilder.com

DISCLAIMER
While all reasonable precautions were made to ensure the accuracy of material contained in this publication, it is a condition of purchase that the publishers do not assume any responsibility for any loss or damage which may result from any inaccuracy or omission in this publication, or from the use or reliance upon the information contained herein. The publishers make no warranties, express or implied, with respect to any of the material contained in the publication.

Published by Kester Marketing PO Box 3119, Wheeler's Hill, Victoria 3150 Australia. info@kestermarketing.com.au

Table of Contents

INTRODUCTION 1
FOREWORD 2
PREFACE 3
HOW TO USE MARKETING PLAN BUILDER 4
INTRODUCTORY NOTES 6
EXECUTIVE SUMMARY 16
CHAPTER 1. SALES & MARKET REVIEW 17
1.1 Sales Analysis 18
1.2 Products or Services Review 21
1.3 Market Segmentation 22
1.4 Product (or Service) Segmentation 23
1.5 Competitor Analysis 26
1.6 Marketing Research 29
CHAPTER 2. SITUATION ANALYSIS 32
2.1 SWOT Analysis 32
2.2 Mission Statement 35
2.3 Target Markets 37
2.4 Keys to Success 39
2.5 Critical Issues 40
CHAPTER 3. MARKETING AND SALES OBJECTIVES 42
3.1 Marketing Objectives 42
3.2 Sales Objectives 44
CHAPTER 4. MARKETING STRATEGIES 45
PRODUCT 46
4.1.1 Product (or Service) Development 46
4.1.2 Product Proposition 49
4.1.3 Positioning 51
4.1.4 Branding 54
4.1.5 Brand & Corporate Image 56
4.1.6 Packaging 58
PRICE 59
4.2.1 Price Strategies 61
4.2.2 Price Tactics 63
PLACE 64
4.3.1 Business Location 64
4.3.2 Distribution 66
4.3.3 Distribution Channel Partners Business Maximization . . 68
4.3.4 Supply Chain Management 69

PROMOTION ... 71
4.4.1 Sales Force Management ... 71
4.4.2 Sales Development ... 73
4.4.3 Customer Service ... 76
4.5 Advertising ... 79
4.5.1 Setting the Advertising Objectives ... 80
4.5.2 Advertising Responsibilities Allocation ... 81
4.5.3 Setting the Advertising Budget ... 82
4.5.4 Preparing the Creative Brief and Execution Evaluation ... 83
4.5.5 Media Selection ... 85
4.5.6 Advertising Research ... 88
4.6 Sales Promotion ... 89
4.7 Trade Shows and Exhibitions ... 92
4.8 On-line Marketing and eCommerce ... 93
4.8.1 Website Functionality ... 94
4.8.2 Website Promotion Strategies ... 96
4.8.3 Social Media Marketing ... 98
4.9 Merchandising ... 100
4.10 Public Relations and Publicity ... 102
4.11 Sponsorship ... 105
4.12 Corporate Communications ... 106
4.13 Direct Marketing and Database Marketing ... 108
CHAPTER 5. FINANCIAL STATEMENTS ... 112
5.1 Marketing Budget ... 112
5.2 Marketing Financial Statement ... 114
CHAPTER 6. IMPLEMENTATION AND CONTROLS ... 116
6.1 Sales & Marketing Personnel Resources ... 116
6.2 Action Plan ... 117
6.3 Implementation Schedule ... 118
6.4 Review & Evaluation Schedule ... 120
Executive Summary ... 122
APPENDIX - CONSOLIDATED SAMPLE MARKETING PLAN ... 123
GLOSSARY ... 176
THE NEXT STEPS ... 182
ABOUT THE AUTHOR ... 183
Index ... 184

> *Marketing is so basic it cannot be considered a separate function. It is the whole business seen from the point of view of its final result, that is, from the customer's point of view. - Peter Drucker*

INTRODUCTION

You do not need to be a marketing professional or even have specialized training in the field to write a plan that will produce a significantly improved outcome. You *do* need a passion for your business and the industry in which you compete, combined with an understanding of the content you need to consider in your plan and the structure you should follow to develop a series of synchronized strategies that can lift your enterprise to the next more profitable stage of development.

This template based book gives you those building blocks in a logical step-by-step process to produce a professional marketing plan that will guide you to realizing your business' full potential.

A marketing plan will:
Identify opportunities in the marketplace that your business can profitably pursue
Increase your productivity through reducing wasted time and effort
Help you concentrate on the things you do best
Improve utilization of your finite resources.
Coordinate every function in your business so that each part is contributing toward the same goals
Provide you with practical day-to-day decision reference points
Sharpen the focus of your business for your customers and employees
Give you a clear advantage on your nearest competitors
Drive profitable growth
Give your business the tools required to reach its full potential

'With a cohesive, strategic marketing plan in place, you can systematically develop your business for a more profitable outcome'

A marketing plan does not necessarily require a need to spend more for an improved outcome. The mere process of systematically thinking through your business to ensure you are selling the right products or services, to the right people, in the right place at the right price and at the right time, will set you on the path to a more productive and profitable end result.

Put every piece of your marketing plan in place with this easy-to-follow step-by-step process

FOREWORD

This guide to writing a marketing plan that will leverage your business to the next more profitable stage of development takes you through the process step-by-step. It is particularly suitable to meet the needs of small to medium enterprises (SME's) although the same principles apply to businesses of all sizes and classes.

The format is appropriate for start-up and established businesses and both business to consumer (B2C) and business to business (B2B) enterprises. The degree of emphasis on sections of the plan will vary from one case to another dependent upon whether the plan is for a product or service based business and the stage of development the business has reached. Therefore there is ample scope for flexibility and discretion in completing the templates provided.

In developing your plan, remember that a sound plan builds on what you have done and learned from in the past, as this is the best guide you can have to what you need to do in the future.

Do not be deterred with the thought that you need to write a huge document. The more concise the plan, the better it will serve you. The plan needs only to be a succinct summary of what you want to achieve and how you are going to reach the goals you have set.

Bear in mind that a marketing plan is a working document providing you with an ongoing reference. When completed, do not bury it in a drawer to gather dust but use it as an integral part of the day-to-day decision making process in managing your business.

Contrary to popular belief, you do not necessarily have to spend more to produce an improved outcome. The mere process of thinking through your objectives and strategies and reshaping them appropriately can set you on a more effective and profitable path.

And bear in mind there is no such thing as 'one plan fits all' as no two sets of circumstances are the same. Writing an effective plan is a thought provoking process. The better the quality of thought that goes into its preparation, the better it will serve you.

You will also find that the plan will create a mind-set, which will make you more aware of opportunities that arise, and how you can capitalise on them.

Just as the dynamics of the market keep changing and as your business progresses, so the plan should be periodically updated to keep abreast of those changes.

Of paramount importance, remember that a marketing plan is not an end in itself but merely a means to an end in setting up the processes that have the potential to drive your business to the next stage in its development. After all, a plan is a working document and is meaningless until it is implemented, and then and only then, it becomes a conduit to a progressively more profitable and rewarding future.

"A plan sets up the processes that deliver the desired results"

PREFACE

In the course of a lifelong career in which I have followed a passion for the pursuit of excellence in all facets of marketing, in all manner of business models and industries, I never cease to be surprised at the way in which countless business owners and operators are frantically engaged in the day-to-day running of their businesses without so much as a basic plan in their minds – let alone committing one to paper.

In the absence of a plan most operators are merely spinning around in ever diminishing circles working *in* their businesses instead of *on* them.

It is almost impossible to achieve anything of significance without devising a plan and putting it into practice. Running a business successfully is not something you can effectively do 'in your head' or 'on the run'. And there is no such thing as 'one plan fits all'.

A plan provides a blueprint to follow without continually having to grapple with strategic decisions and in the process, improves utilization of finite resources. It gives a business the tools required to take it to the next level.

There is no getting away from the fact that assembling a plan is a painstaking exercise that requires considerable time, thought and effort, but the more consideration given to its development, the better it will serve you and the more time it will save you in the long run.

The mere process of planning and analysis that goes into the development of a marketing plan is every bit as important as the plan itself.

Many business operators may very well be highly skilled in their trades and professions but are either not cognizant of the benefits to be gained from devising a plan or do not quite know where to start in developing one. Consequently the task is often never done.

This book is intended to remedy that situation.

Elementary marketing principles and practices are explained and the tools, structure and framework needed to devise a professional plan are provided. Practical tips, ideas and suggestions are given to develop a plan from the ground up that will give every business sharper focus and direction to reach its full potential

I wish the readers of this book the immense satisfaction to be gained from reaching that ultimate goal.

GARTH KESTER
Author *MARKETING PLAN BUILDER*

"A goal without a plan is just a dream" — Dave Ramsay

HOW TO USE MARKETING PLAN BUILDER

Step 1 – Gain a sound working knowledge of the contents of this book

This book guides you through the essential components of a marketing plan and explains elementary marketing principles and practices. It includes tips and suggestions to help you develop a plan that matches the specific needs of your business. A series of completed template examples culminate in a consolidated sample marketing plan.

Because no two businesses are the same the book includes reference keys at each section of the plan (see example below) to indicate the suitability of each step for your business depending on whether you market products or services from business to consumer (B2C) or business to business (B2B).

The reference keys also indicate the applicability of each step according to your plan level preferences from 'Basic' through to "Intermediate' and 'Advanced'.

Reference key example:

Business class	B2C Products ✓	B2B Products ✓	B2C Services ✓	B2B Services ✓
Plan level	Basic ✓		Intermediate ✓	Advanced ✓

Step 2– Build your plan in the free Microsoft ® Word ™ pre-formatted templates [1]

To download the free Microsoft Word document *Marketing Plan Builder templates* go to *www.marketingplanbuilder.com* then scroll down to the link at the foot of the home page. When downloaded go to View > Edit. Then begin the process of documenting your plan by 'filling in the blanks' in the templates supplied. At each step there are pointers, to remind you of the content applicable to that step as well as reference keys to help you determine which templates are relevant to your business class and the plan level you wish to complete.

It is recommended that you copy and paste the individual templates selected for your plan into a clean Microsoft Word document with a separate page for each template. (This will avoid any formatting or layout issues)

When you have completed the selected templates, with any relevant commentary you may wish to add, complete the formatting to your personal preferences.

It is suggested that you develop your plan in manageable 'bite sized chunks'. Fill-in the templates to the 'basic' stage initially, then go on to the more 'intermediate' or 'advanced' stages as your knowledge of the planning process grows and as your understanding of the market in which you are competing increases.

Try to get into the habit of allocating an hour a day to develop the plan. You will

---

[1] You will need Microsoft Word installed in your system and have at least a working knowledge of the program. Depending on your version of the program installed you may need to re-format or re-create some of the templates if compatibility issues occur.

be rewarded with the realization of how much your understanding of the market and your business grow as you progress through the planning process.

On completion you will be ready to start implementing the plan that will produce a vastly improved outcome.

Successful and profitable marketing!

"The more concise a marketing plan is — the better it will serve you"

INTRODUCTORY NOTES

Marketing explained

What is 'marketing' exactly? Common perceptions of the term often confuse different individual components of the 'marketing mix' with the function as a whole. The precise meaning of marketing is the integration of *all* of the individual components of the 'marketing mix' which, when blended together, provides the framework for an enterprise or organization to function more efficiently and more profitably.

> "Integrated marketing communications is a way of looking at the whole marketing communications process from the viewpoint of the customer"
>
> Philip Kotler
> Noted US marketing academic and author

Each part of the mix is a specialized function in its own right. The component parts include such diverse but complementary business activities as product development, advertising, sales, merchandising, publicity, promotions, pricing, packaging, market research, distribution, branding and customer service to name just a few. These are *branches* or *elements* of marketing all of which are constantly evolving as new technologies and trends evolve.

DEFINITIONS

> "Marketing is the total management process in which goods and services are sold in the marketplace. This includes all aspects of planning, strategy development and implementation".

And...

> "Marketing is the determination of end users needs and wants with the development of fulfilment solutions that are communicated to the target market, so that sales are produced for a profitable outcome".

Marketers have been described as 'mixers of ingredients' and have many tools at their disposal and a vast array of options to work with when putting all the pieces of a cohesive marketing plan together.

Essentially, businesses with a marketing focus are *customer* - not *production* driven. It is not about what the factory can produce but what the customer wants or needs. This is the difference between marketing and production driven orientation. The first principle of marketing is: "The customer is pivotal to the process."

Maintaining a customer focus is an essential tenet of marketing. It is a cultivated mind-set – a commitment to delivering value to customers and the development of a sustainable competitive advantage.

This advantage may be created in many different tangible and intangible ways such as a better product, lower prices, improved value, superior quality, advanced technology, wider availability, better service, improved packaging or perhaps conveying a desirable statement or image upon the user, to mention just a few.

The creation of such competitive advantages stem from a thorough understanding of customers, competitors, technology and your own organization's capabilities.

Customer focus is the cornerstone of every successful business's thinking.

You need to understand how your customers think and what they want in a product or service. The opposite of this is to churn out products without considering what customers' actually want.[1]

Marketing is an attitude that becomes part of the corporate culture - not just in marketing and sales departments but throughout the entire organisation. It is a discipline that dictates the need to keep ahead of competitors through ongoing market and marketing research, keeping abreast of local and overseas trends and most importantly - listening to feedback from sales people at the coal face, intermediaries such as wholesalers and retailers and above all — your customers.

Marketing recognizes that people buy solutions to problems to satisfy needs and wants. Consumers don't buy products or services per se unless they provide solutions - even solutions as basic as satisfying human needs as food, clothing and shelter.

Marketing is neither an art nor a science although it has elements of both. It combines tried and tested principles with creative ideas, entrepreneurship and controlled intuition. This calls for a blend of analytical skills, creative flair and a strategic mind-set.

The military analogy

"Marketing is merely a civilised form of warfare in which most battles are won with words, ideas and disciplined thinking". Albert Emery. US advertising executive

Marketing is concerned with gathering intelligence (market research) on the enemy (competitors), developing strategies and tactics, marshalling resources (financial and human), identifying prime targets, mounting attacks and counter attacks (marketing strategies), developing arsenals (marketing tools) and occupying territories (markets or product segments).

In military terms the primary strategies are: offensive, defensive, guerrilla and retreat. The parallels with marketing are striking. Just as a General plans strategies and tactics and marshals his forces, a marketing executive coordinates the direction and thrust for his or her business.

Military campaigns are won through having superior planning and intelligence than your enemy. Equally – market leadership is achieved through having superior market research and a sharper strategic direction than your competitors.

Marketing was once like conventional warfare in that it mainly used mass media just as cannons and bombs were used by the military. Today in this digital age present day marketers use more targeted communications that are the equivalent of modern warfare's smart bombs.

---

1. This practice was termed Marketing Myopia by Theodore Levitt in a seminal article in Harvard Businesss Review in 1960.

What can a marketing plan do for your business?

Most of us would not attempt to build even a simple garden shed without at least a basic plan to follow. Successful teams in any sport have a game plan. Military commanders devise battle plans. Successful people devise career plans. In short, you cannot do anything effectively without some kind of plan in place. Yet it is a fact that the majority of small to medium enterprises operate without even an elementary plan in their mind – let alone on paper.

Without a written cohesive marketing plan, you and your business are probably spinning around in ever diminishing circles with the result that your enterprise has little hope of ever reaching its full potential. Running a successful business is not something you can do effectively without system or structure.

It does not have to be a complicated process. A plan simply gives you the tools to build your business methodically and to allow you to concentrate on the skills in which you and your business do best. It gives you an edge over others who do not have a plan and are competing for the same customers.

A marketing plan lays out the steps your company will take to achieve your sales and marketing goals.

Without a marketing plan, you are merely busily processing random activity.

With a plan in place you are taking a disciplined approach to thinking through your products and services, your customers and prospects and to developing effective strategies that achieve realistic, attainable goals.

A marketing plan enables you to focus on your strengths and reduces wasted time and effort. It will help you to concentrate on the most profitable outcome for the least amount of investment. It heeds the golden rule, *"do not fritter money or effort"*.

Involving your key people in "work shopping" the plan is a good way to gain their thinking, commitment and "ownership" of the plan.

The time spent in planning and analysis that goes into a marketing plan is *every bit as important as the plan itself.*

Remember "everyone can profit from working *on* your business – not just *in* your business". But to do so you need to make the time to analyze what you are doing and to take an overview of the business as a whole. You should try to approach it as objectively and dispassionately as if you were external to the company.

Build your plan in three systematic stages

1. Where are we now? (Market & Sales Review and Situation Analysis)

This is an analysis of the current status of your products or services both in relation to the rate of sales growth and profitability and potential for future growth. This requires analysis of your sales records and accounts.

The next step is to determine where your business, product or service lies in relation to the market in which you compete. Are you in a growth or declining market?

Are you favorably placed to grow your share of market? Are you going to create an entirely new market segment? Where are the gaps? What opportunities are there to take advantage of? This process involves conducting a systematic review of the market in which you compete.

2. Where do we want to go? (Marketing & Sales Objectives)

This step involves the determination of the direction in which you want to steer the business. It follows the analysis stage, which has led you to make certain conclusions about opportunities and feasibilities. At this point you define your sales and marketing objectives. In many ways this is the most difficult part of putting your plan together as it requires considerable thought in regard to what is both practical and desirable and making a commitment to achieving the set goals and targets.

3. How are we going to get there? (Marketing Strategies, Financial Statements and Implementation Controls)

Now that you know 'where you are' and 'where you want to go', determining 'how you are going to get there' becomes much more straightforward than just having a vague idea in your head about what you need to do to get the desired results.

This stage of the plan requires devising and implementing the strategies you need to achieve the set objectives and the determination of the financial and human resources you will need to put the selected strategies in place.

Marketing plans, business plans and strategic plans

Marketing, business plans and strategic plans are closely related and have extensive overlap. They differ in purposes, perspectives and emphasis.

Business plans have three main components: a marketing plan, an operational plan and a financial plan.

The operational plan examines such considerations as supply sources, costs, staffing and equipment and so on.

The financial plan shows all the numbers affecting the business including a cash flow forecast, balance sheet, profit and loss statement, sources of funding and tax statements.

The business plan deals with the broader background in which the marketing plan can reach fruition. That is why the two must be compatible. A business plan is often used to obtain finance or venture capital from a bank, shareholders or other investors. It encompasses marketing but also addresses finance, production and administration.

A formal business plan should project three to five years in the future, outlining the route a company intends to take to reach its yearly milestones, including revenue projections.

Marketing plans are often part of a broader business plan but the two are not mutually exclusive. A marketing plan can be for a single product or service or for a group of products or services. The period most marketing plans cover is one year as it is difficult to look ahead much further than that as changes in the market occur constantly. Once written, you should update the plan each year mindful of the changes to the market and your own business that have occurred since the plan was developed.

The marketing plan looks at what a business sells, its location, packaging, pricing and selling methods. Anything connected with "selling" your products or services forms part of the marketing plan. A marketing plan is more comprehensive on anything to do with selling your products or services than the contents of the marketing section of a business plan.

Strategic plans take more of an overview and longer-term view – usually between five and ten years. They have a lot to do with where your company is now, your vision for the future, and how you are going to get there. It addresses marketing, operations, innovation (including services offered and technology needed), human resources and finance.

Market research and *marketing* research

Market research is the process of researching the size, shape and trends of a specific market. (Such as the market for office furniture, infants clothing, courier services, etc.). Market research is secondary research (also known as desk research) which involves the collection and analysis of existing information such as your internal sales history and external data, much of which is freely accessible on the Internet.

Marketing research on the other hand is primary research (also known as field research). It involves the collection of data that does not already exist and is specially commissioned (and usually paid for) by you to obtain essential information on considerations that may include different aspects of consumer behavior such as likes and dislikes, where and how frequently they buy, how they regard your products compared with competitors, what would influence them to change their current behavior and so on.

Some level of both market and marketing research is essential information to have before you can begin to think about what your objectives should be and what strategies you need to devise to achieve them. To the extent that it is reasonably practical, your plan must ultimately be based on facts, not wishful thinking.

Ideally, marketing plans should begin and end with marketing research. First, you research what you *should* be doing. Then after implementation you research to determine if you have achieved what you set out to do.

You cannot know too much about your customers and prospects. Facts and figures are much better than guesses and estimates. There is no substitute for hard data although when these are not available, informed estimates are better than nothing.

You have to know how your customers and potential customers perceive the value of your products and services to make good marketing decisions. If you don't know how your company and its products are perceived, you risk wasting time and aiming the wrong products at the wrong markets at the wrong time.

TABLE 1. Marketing research techniques				
Research Technique	How Conducted	Advantages	Disadvantages	Quantitative or Qualitative
Personal interviews	Trained interviewer completes structured questionnaire face to face with respondents who are a representative sample of the target market.	Good ability to control. The interviewer can clarify any queries or misunderstandings on the spot. Statistically significant if sufficient respondents.	Expensive to recruit and interview respondents. Respondents often relate what they think you want to hear.	Can be both quantitative and qualitative depending on scale
Telephone surveys	Trained interviewer completes structured questionnaire in telephone conversations with respondents	Logistically less expensive to conduct than personal interviews. Can be structured to be statistically significant.	Not suitable for long probing interviews. Respondents often uncooperative and impatient	As above
On-line surveys	Respondents complete web based questionnaires	Cost efficient and conducted in 'real time'. Can be structured to be statistically significant. Ideal for customer feedback.	Low participation rate unless respondents have a keen interest in the product category or offered incentive to participate..	As above
Mail surveys	Questionnaires circulated and returned by mail. Self-completed by respondents	Respondents can complete in own time. Can be structured to be statistically significant.	Postage and administration costs can mount up. Low participation rate. Completed without supervision.	As above
Field surveys	Observation of actual consumer behavior and retail conditions in shops and stores	Research is conducted in a 'real world" (not artificial) environment.	Can be very subjective. Not statistically valid.	Qualitative
Focus groups	Trained moderator leads a series of group discussions of up to 12 respondents each whom are representative of the target market	Opportunities to probe. Identifies areas of interest for further probing and research	Requires expert facilitation. High recruitment costs. Not statistically significant.	Qualitative

Advertising agencies or do it yourself?

Advertising is just one of many marketing disciplines and it can occupy a central role in the strategic development process. This leads to the question: how are you going to plan and implement your advertising? Do you engage the services of an advertising agency, coordinate one or more independent specialists or do it yourself?

As a general rule the services of advertising agencies are cost prohibitive for most SME's. Many large agencies will not accept an account with billings of less than six figures ($US) per annum. Smaller agencies will want a regular income stream at the very least.

Appointing an advertising agency

Assuming the availability of a substantial advertising budget the process of agency selection can be complex and time consuming. It is often worthwhile to talk to suppliers and other network contacts to obtain referrals and personal recommendations before compiling a 'short list' from which you could invite two or three candidates to make speculative creative submissions.

From these you can assess which one you feel comfortable working with and which meets the brief most closely and creatively. Advertising agency relationships should be looked at as long term so it is important to get the selection process 'right' in the first instance.

Agency remuneration

There are various methods of setting agency remuneration. The most common is a combination of media commissions (paid by the medium with which the advertising is placed - usually around 10% of billings) plus additional fees paid by the advertiser (ranging from around 5 to 10% of media billings).

Many advertisers argue that this method is inequitable, as it bears no relationship with the amount of work undertaken and encourages agencies to consciously or not propose self-serving increases in media spending.

The fee system has become increasingly popular among advertisers. When a program has been agreed a 'set fee' is negotiated based on the amount of work required. In this scenario media commissions are rebated to the advertiser either in part or in full. This is sometimes augmented with an additional media placement fee of a percentage of gross media billings to cover media planning, negotiation and placement.

A recent trend is to negotiate performance based compensation based on sales or market share results. This concept is an over simplification for many advertisers because of the many variables involved which make it almost impossible to accurately identify cause and effect however there are KPI's (such as advertising awareness and recall measurements) that can be integrated in an agreed formula.

Developing advertising 'in-house'

Coordinating your advertising yourself is a more practical approach for most small businesses. Producing advertising without an advertising agency need not be the same as 'doing it yourself'. In the past many companies such as large retail chains elected to have in-house advertising departments but this has now largely had its day because of prohibitive overhead costs.

A more practical and less expensive approach is to outsource or 'farm out' the services you require to independent specialists such as freelance copywriters, graphic artists, web designers, photographers, or studios that offer a comprehensive service.

You can also enlist the services of the publication or station with which the advertising is placed to help you create the advertising material. Printers, newspapers, magazines, outdoor advertising firms and radio and TV stations often offer these services free or at a reasonable cost.

When the advertising material is produced, media placement can either be handled by placing a schedule with the publication or station directly or, if the size of the budget warrants, through specialized media buying services or consultants.

Another practical option is to engage the services of an independent marketing consultant to assist you with planning, coordinating and implementing your entire advertising program.

Product life cycles

Most product categories have life cycles, that is to say they will eventually be replaced by products that evolve because of changing technology or fashion. Before formulating your strategies under the 4P's, (Product, Place, Price and Promotion) you should first consider where your product or service is in its' life cycle. When exploring what mix is most appropriate consider which of the following phases is appropriate to your product or product category.

Introductory Phase

If you are releasing a brand new product or service to the market your product, price, place and promotion strategies are critical considerations. If they are not competitive and different enough from the offerings already available, the chances of your product becoming established are not good.

Growth Phase

If you have been enjoying a degree of exclusivity and comparative success, be prepared for competitive 'me too' products. How you react to competition will impact your survival. Will you reduce your prices, change the way in which you promote your product or change or expand your channels of distribution.

Maturity Phase

If your product is a 'me too' product competing for the same customers as other products your product has reached the maturity phase. This phase has its own set of complications as your product is vulnerable to being swamped by competitors. You will need to carefully consider changes to your marketing strategies, including updating the product itself, so you can adapt to changing circumstances.

Decline Phase

If sales are static or falling your product may be close to or at the end of its life cycle. Technology based products are especially prone to short life cycles. Consider how email has replaced fax machines, how DVD and Blu-ray players have made VCR's redundant and how iPods and smartphones have replaced Sony Walkmans. If this applies to your product category you should consider 'milking' the product for any remaining revenue, re-invent it through changes to branding, presentation or packaging; repositioning it to a different target market, or if it is not profitable take the decision to delete it from your product range. Even if products have been very successful in the past there is no place for sentiment in business if they are no longer contributing to profitable revenue.

The new paradigm in marketing

The phenomenal pace of change in web based or digital marketing has caught some 'traditional' marketers by surprise.

Digital marketing is the marketing of products or services using digital technologies, mainly on the Internet but also including mobile phones, display advertising on third part web sites and any other digital medium.

Now, more than ever, consumers are empowered with instant access to information about products and services through 'inbound marketing' strategies such as blogs, podcasts, enewsletters, eBooks, webinars, social media marketing, viral marketing, and online videos. Digital technology has truly created a dramatic shift in marketing emphasis. The development is so profound that many businesses now employ specialist digital marketers.

These tools have not replaced 'outbound marketing' mass media such as TV, radio, billboards print ads and the like, but provide exciting new avenues to reach target audiences with more precision and often at a fraction of the cost.

The challenge to marketers today is to keep abreast of these rapidly evolving trends and to constantly adapt marketing strategies and tactics so that the right balance is struck between traditional and digital marketing.

> **❝** *The challenge is to strike the perfect balance between 'traditional' and digital marketing* **❞**

Marketing plan elements

The component parts of marketing plans should be tailored to suit the needs of individual businesses. Most advanced marketing plans will include all of the elements listed below. Basic and intermediate marketing plans will comprise selected elements as denoted by the reference keys included in each section in this book. Use the headings in the table below as a checklist when building your plan.

TABLE 2. Marketing plan elements checklist	
1. EXECUTIVE SUMMARY	Marketing strategies (continued).
2. SALES & MARKET REVIEW	PLACE
Sales Analysis	Business location
Products or services review	Distribution
Market segmentation	Distribution channels maximization
Product or service segmentation	Supply chain management
Competitive analysis	PROMOTION
Marketing research	Sales force management
3. SITUATION ANALYSIS	Sales development
SWOT analysis	Customer service
Mission statement	Advertising
Target markets	Sales promotion
Keys to success	Trade shows & exhibitions
Critical issues	Online marketing & e-commerce
4. MARKETING & SALES OBJECTIVES	Website functionality & promotion
Marketing objectives	Social media marketing
Sales objectives	Merchandising
5. MARKETING STRATEGIES	Public relations & publicity
PRODUCT	Sponsorship
Product development	Corporate communications
Product proposition	Direct and database marketing
Positioning	6. FINANCIAL STATEMENTS
Branding	Marketing budget
Brand & corporate image	Financial statement
Packaging	7. IMPLEMENTATION & CONTROLS
PRICE	Sales & marketing human resources
Pricing strategies	Action plan
Pricing tactics	Implementation schedule
Go to next column >>	Review & evaluation schedule

EXECUTIVE SUMMARY

The purpose of the executive summary of the marketing plan is to provide the reader with an overview explaining where your business has been and where it is going as a result of the strategies developed in the plan. It provides a synopsis of:

- When and why the business was established and the markets it was set up to enter.
- A description of the products or services you offer
- A brief profile of your trade and end-user customers
- A summary of your progress in the market to date and obstacles encountered
- The dynamics that have arisen that need to be addressed
- A summary of the main factors in the plan that will lead to forecast sales and profits. This could include such considerations as the identification of new market opportunities, increased or more efficient utilization of advertising or promotional expenditure or more efficient distribution or product development that will appeal more to your target markets than competitive products.
- The impact the plan will have on your top (sales) and bottom (profit) lines.

While the executive summary appears at the start of the plan it cannot be completed until all the parts of the plan are in place. So leave this part of the plan until the rest of the plan is finalized. (See executive summary Template 57).

The executive summary provides an overview of the thrust, reasoning and expected outcome of the plan

CHAPTER 1. SALES & MARKET REVIEW

Before setting out to develop the plan you need to have a thorough understanding of your company's recent sales history, your position in the market segment and the size, shape and state of the market in which you compete. This is sometimes referred to as 'a sales and market audit' which reflects 'where you are' as the first step in determining 'where you want to go'.

You cannot know too much about your customers and prospects. Facts and figures make the difference between a plan that is realistic and objective and one that is subjective and fanciful.

Ideally, you should have at least a broad understanding of:
A profile of your company's sales history over at least the last three years with an understanding of which products are growing or declining and contributing to your gross and net profit.
The value and volume of the market in which you compete [1]
The growth sectors of the market
An estimate of product segment shares, of the total market
A trade profile of the market
A profile of end users or consumers

With this knowledge you can assess your current market position, define where you want to be and understand the problems and opportunities that are presented.

A wealth of information can be gathered from such external sources as:
- The Internet
- Government bureaus or instrumentalities [2]
- Trade publications
- Trade and industry associations
- Public libraries
- Annual reports
- Market research firms
- The Yellow Pages and other trade directories.

---

1. The figures on market size are not meaningful when the business is a small fish in a very large pond. For example an accounting firm will derive no benefit from knowing the size of the national accounting market. But it would be helpful to know the size of the market in their localized area and how many firms there are competing for this business. Trade associations and on-line directories (such as Yellow Pages) are often good reference sources from which to gather this information.
2. For example US Census Bureau/Business Bureau / UK Office for National Statistics / Australian Bureau of Statistics (ABS)

Your own internal sales records can be a rich source of untapped information and is invariably the best place to start.

The Internet is invaluable to establish what external information exists. Some may be available at no cost or for just a moderate outlay. More detailed data may cost more but it could be very useful in helping you to analyze market opportunities that would otherwise not be possible.

If hard market data is not readily available, projections or estimates based on anecdotal evidence is an acceptable starting point.

At the very least you need to know which product or service categories are growing, declining or remaining the same.

You can always update estimates as pieces of hard data become available to allow you to piece the picture together. At times, it is possible to gather a reasonably accurate estimate of the big picture from fragments of information collected from a variety of collaborative or anecdotal sources. When using data in a plan to support a conclusion or a course of action it is good practice to quote the source of the data.

1.1 Sales Analysis

Business class	B2C Products ✔	B2B Products ✔	B2C Services ✔	B2B Services ✔
Plan level	Basic ✔	Intermediate ✔	Advanced ✔	

An analysis of your own sales records is the logical place to start the planning process. Ideally this should comprise a review of your individual products or services over the last three years showing:
- Turnover
- Gross profit before expenses
- Net profit (or loss)

When you have completed the analysis you will have a better understanding of which products' sales have grown, declined or stayed about the same in the period.

If the data is available you can also track each products contribution to gross and/or net profit or loss. You may be surprised to find that some products are actually making a loss in which case you should give serious consideration to deleting them from the range.

This section of your marketing plan should include a commentary giving an explanation for the trends such as increased competition, a declining market or depressed economic conditions.

This information aids in the classification of your products into one of four groups in a simple matrix that allows you to view your product portfolio at a glance: (Refer Boston Consulting Group Matrix page 20)

Cash cows are low maintenance established products that provide cash flow and profit for investment in other areas such as new product development.

Template 1 – Company sales analysis by product or service (example)

	Turnover $000s			Gross Profit or Loss $000s			Net Profit or loss $000s		
Product or Service	3 years ago	2 years ago	Last year	3 years ago	2 years ago	Last year	3 years ago	2 years ago	Last year
Executive desks, returns & screens	1,300	1,200	1,100	715	660	605	286	264	242
Bookcases	110	105	100	55	50	45	22	21	20
Office chairs	210	200	190	105	100	95	42	40	35
Office tables	300	290	280	150	145	140	60	55	50
Filing cabinets	150	140	150	30	28	30	(15)	(14)	(15)
Total	2,070	1,935	1,820	1055	983	915	395	366	332

Conclusion: Sales of our entire product range are flat or in slow decline. We need to develop new products for future sustainable growth as a matter of urgency!

Dogs make a negative contribution to profit and should be deleted from the product range unless they fill some strong strategic purpose such as keeping you involved with customers that would otherwise not deal with you.

Rising stars are products that are rapidly gathering sales and profit momentum. Bright future - but require high investment.

Question marks have the potential to become any one of the three other classifications and should be analyzed carefully in order to determine whether they are worth the investment required to gain market share.

Template 2. - Product or service classifications (example)

Boston Consulting Group Matrix[1]

Market growth rate: High

Rising Stars

Stars are products that are rapidly gathering sales and profit momentum. Bright future - but require high investment

We have no products in this prized category. Clearly this situation needs to be urgently addressed

Question Marks

Question marks have the potential to become stars, cows, or dogs and must be analyzed carefully in order to determine whether they are worth the investment required to grow market share

● Bookcases & office chairs.

Market growth rate: Low

Cash Cows

Cash cows are low maintenance established products that should be 'milked' to provide cash flow and profit for investment in other areas such as new product development.

● Executive desks & tables

Dogs

Dogs make a negative contribution to profit and should be deleted from the product range unless they fill some strong strategic purpose such as keeping you involved with customers who would otherwise not deal with you.

● Filing cabinets

Market share: High — Low

---

[1] The BCG matrix was created by Bruce Henderson of the Boston Consulting Group in 1970 as an aid to analyzing business units or product lines.

1.2 Products or Services Review

Business class	B2C Products ✓	B2B Products ✓	B2C Services ✓	B2B Services ✓
Plan level	Basic ✓	Intermediate ✓		Advanced ✓

A key part of the initial analysis process is getting to know your existing products and services better than the competition knows theirs.

- What are the benefits of your products and services?
- How do your products compare with your competitors?
- What product or service is the best contributor to your overheads and profits?
- What is the status of each product or service in terms of market growth potential and market share?

If you are just selling 'me too' products without any real or perceived benefits, your business is in danger of being overtaken by your competitors.

Template 3 - Existing products or services review (example)

Product or Service	Benefits	Comparison with competitors	Profit contributor rating (1 – 10)	Product or service classification (Refer Template 2)
Executive desks, returns & Screens	High quality craftsmanship	Better built than most	10	Cash cows but under threat
Bookcases	Easily assembled	Middle quality range	5	Question marks - future doubtful
Office chairs	Gas lifts	No clear advantage	4	Question marks - limited growth opportunity
Office tables	Solid timber	High quality end of market	6	Cash cow but slowing demand
Filing cabinets	Fully welded	In most expensive quartile	3	Dogs - losing money but completes a range

"Ask yourself - what is your competitive edge?"

1.3 Market Segmentation

Business class	B2C Products ✔	B2B Products ✔	B2C Services ✔	B2B Services ✔
Plan level	Basic ✔	Intermediate ✔		Advanced ✔

Definition: *Market segmentation is the process of dividing a market into distinct and meaningful groups of buyers who merit separate products and marketing.*

Your business has a potential market consisting of a vaguely defined group of people who might buy your products. To invest your money wisely you have to narrow that broad group down to those people most likely to buy from you.

Customer focus forces your business to succeed.

All markets can be divided into smaller groups or "market segments".

If you do this with the market in which you are competing it will help you to develop your plans and to competitively position your products or services.

Market segmentation is a method of organizing and categorizing those people or organizations that you think will buy your products. You are breaking the market down into smaller and smaller units to make your planning simpler and more effective.

A market segmentation analysis will help you to determine to whom you can sell most profitably. Think of the 80/20 rule: 80 per cent of your profits come from 20 per cent of your customers.

Each market segment meets different needs and has different characteristics to the others.

You can define market segments by groups of customer types. For example if you are an office furniture manufacturer you could segment the market into four primary groups.

TABLE 3. Market Segmentation (commercial furniture industry example)	
Large office fit outs	**Large office replacements & additions**
New and refurbished buildings – usually specified by architect or other – purchases direct from manufacturer.	Existing workplaces – purchase from manufacturers direct or from wholesalers or specialist office furniture retailers.
Small office	**Home office**
Fewer than 12 people. Usually purchase from specialist office furniture retailers.	One or two person offices. Usually purchase from general furniture retailers with a limited office furniture section.

To provide another example, a gourmet food manufacturer could segment the market into contract caterers, restaurants, hotels and institutions each of which have different purchasing sources.

When you have identified the market segments applicable to your products or services you can rate the extent to which they are already being catered for, your ability to service the segment, the estimated growth rate of the segment and your level of priority to compete in the segment. You can go on to break down these customer groups into sub-segments (or groups within groups) to sharpen your focus further.

At a later stage you will be able to break your market up further by defining target markets or prime prospects within market segments or sub segments. For example you could refine target markets by demographics and other criteria.

Template 4 - Market segmentation and opportunity rating (example)

Existing & Potential market segments	Rate the extent to which the segment is already being serviced by competitors Scale 1-10	Rate your current or potential ability to service this segment Scale 1-10	Estimated growth rate Scale 1-10	Rate your level of priority Scale 1-10
Large office fit outs	10	0	5	0
Large office replacements	7	2	5	3
Small office	3	8	9	10
Home office	2	10	9	10

Conclusion: Large office fit outs and replacements are already dominated by the large commercial furniture manufacturers. Based on existing competition, our ability to service and estimated growth rates, the small office/home office segments are the segments with the most promising potential in which to concentrate our resources.

1.4 Product (or Service) Segmentation

Definition: *Product or service segmentation is a sub-sector of a larger product category.*

All market segments can be further broken down into product segments In order to sharpen your focus you should have an understanding of what the main product sectors are in the overall market in which you are competing.

For example the pet foods market may be segmented into canned and dry pet foods for dogs and cats.

The desktop printer market can be segmented into laser and inkjet printers stand alone and multifunction devices etc. Convenience foods may be segmented by canned, frozen, dried etc.

The swimming pool market could be segmented into landscaped pools, lap pools, spas, above ground pools, below ground pools, etc.

A home maintenance contractor may segment his market by lawn maintenance, landscaping, garden refuse removal, commercial and domestic, etc.

A fruit juice manufacturer could segment his business by fresh refrigerated products and long shelf life products.

The key principle behind product segmentation is that a company can produce a line of products each with relatively minor variations and target them to different customer groups, sometimes under different brand names, in order to increase overall market share while reducing the cost of developing and manufacturing totally diverse products. This strategy brings into play a diversification of risk (not putting all your eggs in one basket) while providing economies of scale in manufacturing, marketing and distribution.

When you have defined the product sectors that are relevant to your market you should develop an understanding of their sizes and values and where each is in their respective life cycle stage such as growth, maturity or decline phases.

1.4.1 Product or Service Segmentation by Size and Trend

Business class	B2C Products ✔	B2B Products ✔	B2C Services ✔	B2B Services ✔
Plan level	Basic ✔	Intermediate ✔	Advanced ✔	

The first step in product segmentation is to identify all the product categories that are sold to the market segment or segments that you cater for. Then you can refine the market breakdown further by product segment by estimating the size of each segment by volume (in tons, liters, units or other recognized industry measure) and value and rating each segment by its life cycle stage to assess if it is growing or declining. [1] Much of this information can often be gathered cheaply or at no cost from trade associations and on-line directories.

Government statistics statutory offices such as US Census Bureau/Business Bureau /UK Office for National Statistics / Australian Bureau of Statistics (ABS), are also rich sources of industry data.

When you have conducted this exercise a picture will start to emerge as to where the prime growth opportunities are to be found. It would be pointless to invest in a product segment that has peaked and is in the decline stage of its life cycle. (Refer 'Product life cycles' section in introductory notes).

The ultimate aim in this analysis is to identify growth product segments ahead of the competition. To be 'first in' to a product segment is an enormous competitive advantage.

You can always revise or upgrade your product segment estimates as your knowledge of the market grows.

> *You can break product segments down further by segment size and growth (or decline) trend*

---

[1] In the case of small or micro businesses there is no point in estimating the market volume and value of product segments as the national share the business is competing for is not meaningful. It would be helpful however to break up the market by product segment and to have an understanding of which segments are growing and which are declining.

Template 5 - Product segmentation by size and trend (example)

Product segment	Product segment volume (Units)	Product segment value $	Estimated product share of market by value %	Life cycle stage Growth, maturity or decline
1. Work stations	25,000	$50M	26	Rapid Growth
2. Desks	30,000	$75M	39	Mature
3. Returns	5,000	$12M	6	Slow decline
4. Work tables	19,000	$45M	22	Slow Decline
5. Storage units	3,000	$7M	4	Slow Decline
6. Screens	2,000	$5	3	Slow Decline
TOTAL MARKET	84,000	$194M	100	

Key Points: 1. Corporate offices are down sizing due to technology advancements, office rent and labor costs which are influencing a trend away from office desks to workstations. 2. Work stations product segment has grown to become the second largest segment by volume and value. It is the only segment in a rapid growth phase as a result of changing market dynamics.

1.4.2 Product Segmentation by Channels of Distribution

Business class	B2C Products ✔	B2B Products ✔	B2C Services ✘	B2B Services ✘
Plan level	Basic ✘	Intermediate ✘	Advanced ✔	

At an advanced plan level you can refine the market breakdown by product segment further still by drilling down to the main channels of distribution with an estimate of importance (by volume or value) for each product segment in the sector. Rough estimates are better than nothing as you can update them as your knowledge of the market becomes clearer.

You can often get a good idea of a breakdown of product segments by channels of distribution simply by undertaking trade visits for personal observation, talking to your suppliers and customers and by examining your competitors' websites and their advertising and promotional material.

When devising distribution strategies use the current market profile as a benchmark as to what the rest of the industry is doing but do not be obliged to mirror the profile as there may be more creative and competitive courses of action available – particularly in light of the endless opportunities presented by online strategies.

While you are conducting analyses of this type you are gaining a keener appreciation of the market in which you are competing while building a better understanding of where opportunities for growth and development are to be found. You can never know too much about the market in which you are competing.

Template 6 - Product segments by channels of distribution (example)						
Market segment: Small offices/ home offices	Channels of distribution %					
Product segment	Channel 1. Direct from factory	Channel 2. Office furniture manufacturers	Channel 3. Domestic furniture manufacturers	Channel 4. Office Supply Chains	Channel 5. Wholesalers	Channel 6. eCommerce
1. Work stations	10	45	25	12	8	0
2. Desks	20	35	30	10	3	2
3. Returns	20	35	30	10	3	2
4. Work tables	25	35	25	10	3	2
5. Storage units	25	35	20	15	3	2
6. Screens	25	35	25	10	3	2
KEY POINT: Unlike large and medium offices whose office furniture needs are primarily serviced direct from manufacturers, the majority of small office/home office furniture supplies are purchased retail.						

1.5 Competitor Analysis

Business class	B2C Products ✓	B2B Products ✓	B2C Services ✓	B2B Services ✓
Plan level	Basic ✓	Intermediate ✓		Advanced ✓

Competitor analysis is an important part of your marketing plan. You can often learn from your competitors and strengthen your business from the findings. You can assess what they are doing right and what they are not.

As a minimum you need to have an understanding of:

Who are your three or four leading competitors?
What do your competitors do better than you?
What do you do better than you competitors?
What is your competitive position?
What do you need to do to improve your competitive position?

Market shares and annual turnover will be difficult to source in the case of most SME's as this information is rarely published. You can develop rough estimates based on your own business then comparing the number of people employed and their general presence in the market.

Here are some of the techniques you can use to gather intelligence on your main competitors:

Visit their websites. This is the first place to start your research. Websites reveal an enormous amount of information about a business. Posing as a customer you can even use their 'contact us' email facility to ask questions a customer might ask. Also 'Google' key words that are important to your business to see where you rank in the listings compared to your rivals. They may be outdoing you in online marketing and eCommerce.

Visit their premises to gather sales literature and price lists and talk to salesmen. **Inspect** their products in showrooms or retail outlets. Buy samples for more detailed analysis.

Monitor their advertising. Collect clippings of print advertising.

Obtain feedback from customers who may have dealt with competitors.

Talk to your sales force. Ask them to include feedback on competitors in sales reports. They will encounter competitor information almost on a daily basis such as who has quoted for work successfully.

Talk to your suppliers. They service the entire industry in which you compete and have firsthand knowledge of the main players. Suppliers can often be persuaded to impart useful information in the process of gaining business from you.

Industry associations can provide competitor information such as in articles in their publications

Trade directories such as Yellow Pages can often give you the number of entries in an industry by locality. The size of their paid entry will also give you an indication of their relative size.

It can be useful to identify your most successful competitor and use them as a role model upon which to compare your approach to marketing with theirs and to assist in the identification of improvement opportunities.

"You can learn a great deal from your competitors"

Template 7 - Competitor analysis (example)

Criteria	Our company: Wellbuilt	Competitor 1 Name: Premier	Competitor 2 Name Stylecraft	Competitor 3 Name: Colonial	Competitor 4 Name: Nova
Estimated market share	Around 8%	45%	20%	10%	5%
Estimated annual sales	$1,200,000	$7,000,000	$3,000,000	$1,500,000	$700,000
Reputation in market	High end	The industry standard	Solid	Not well defined	Cheap
Price	Premium	High end	Medium to high	Middle range	Low end
Product quality	High	Medium to high	Middle range	Average	Poor
Product range	Comprehensive	Comprehensive	Comprehensive	Limited	Basic
Service	Fair	Excellent	Good	Good	Poor
Location	Prime position to service local market	Central	Acceptable	Acceptable	Poor
Distribution	Patchy	Extensive	Fair	Selective	Poor
Advertising	Limited at present	Prominent	Prominent in local press	None that we can discern	None
Innovation	Lacking to date	Leaders	Usually follow Bettabilt	Nothing to go on recently	Just copies others
Current market segment focus	Large office ad hoc replacement and additions	Large office fit outs and large office ad hoc replacements and additions	Large office ad hoc replacement and additions	Large office ad hoc replacement and additions	Large office ad hoc replacement and additions

KEY POINTS: Based on the competitor analysis above, the reality is that we are currently a small fish in a big pond. Furthermore our share of that pond is contracting due to changing market dynamics. Fortunately, we have identified an underdeveloped market segment in which our competitive position would be that of a bigger fish in a small but growing pond. Our competitive position will be greatly advantaged if we are "first in" to gain leadership of this market segment in our traditional home base.

1.6 Marketing Research

Business class	B2C Products ✔	B2B Products ✔	B2C Services ✔	B2B Services ✔
Plan level	Basic ✘		Intermediate ✔	Advanced ✔

Aspects of market research you have conducted combined with feedback received from your sales force, customers, retailers, suppliers or anyone else who has an interest in your products or services may suggest potential opportunities or 'gaps in the market' that may warrant further investigation.

Before entering into a major commitment of funds to develop new opportunities, you may need to validate your theories, impressions and conclusions. This calls for marketing research or primary research (also known as field research). It involves the collection of data that does not already exist and is specially commissioned (and usually paid for by you) to obtain essential information on considerations that may include different aspects of consumer behavior such as likes and dislikes, where and how frequently they buy, how they regard your products compared with competitors, what would influence them to change their current behavior and so on.

There are many marketing research methods available. (Refer Table 1. Marketing research techniques).

You could conduct a customer survey to assess the level of satisfaction with your products/services among existing users.

You could engage the services of a market research firm to conduct qualitative research focus groups to discuss, attitudes and opinions.

You could appoint the services of a market research firm to conduct statistically valid quantitative surveys with structured questionnaires to establish consumer intentions, propensity to purchase, consumer attitudes to competitive products etc.

Quality marketing research provides information on buyers, products and the competition and gives objective answers to consumers' reactions to product concepts, packaging, advertising and promotion, pricing and almost any other aspect of your marketing mix.

However, do not make the mistake of conducting research just for the sake of it. Some marketers overdo research. Too much research is a waste of time, money and resources and results in 'analysis paralysis'. If you cannot positively act on it once completed – leave it alone!

Before committing funds for major research projects, micro and small businesses in particular can gain invaluable feedback from customers, retailers and suppliers just by taking the time to talk to them over a cup of coffee. Anecdotal evidence costs nothing and can often lead to customer retention and better ways of satisfying your customers' needs and wants.

It is often beneficial to conduct small scale test markets. For example you could test a range of price points in different states, cities or zip codes to see which strategies work best in the 'real world'. This method has the benefit of negligible implementation costs combined with endless permutations of options. You could also test market new product concepts in the same way without committing to full scale production and marketing expenses.

When you strike the best balance between price, sales volume and profitability you can adopt the winning formula on a much larger scale.

Trial and error should be a never ending process in your quest to 'nail' what works best.

Template 8 - Product concept marketing research checklist (example)	
Product concept	High quality/high tech, space efficient, extendable work stations
Market segment	Small offices and home offices
Research objective	Test the validity and the extent to which these market segments offer a viable market opportunity
What we need to know	
Existing behavior	What office furniture equipment are they using now?
Satisfaction with existing products	The extent to which the target market is satisfied/not satisfied with office furniture currently available?
Product needs	What features does the target market require?
Where do they purchase?	Direct from manufacturer? Office furniture retailers? Domestic furniture retailers? Office supplies stores?
How frequently do they purchase?	Periodically? On a needs basis only?
What would influence brand or products switching?	Better functionality? More efficient use of available floor space? Better value for money? Other?
How much are they prepared to pay?	Under $500 per work station. $501 to $750. $751 to $1,000. $1,000 plus.

"Be very selective. Do not make the mistake of conducting research just for the sake of it"

Be wary of anecdotal evidence, especially when it is obtained from uninformed sources. While it can be useful, there is a strong chance that it may be unreliable due to non-representative sample sizes. It can however be used as a starting point to test theories and observations on a more statistically significant scale.

Anecdotal evidence is a form of qualitative data. It's not a measurement of anything, but its very existence tells us that at least one person has perceived something to be true. That's a qualitative data point only, a place to start thinking and asking questions.

"Marketing research can be as basic as talking to your customers and prospects to determine what they think about your products and service"

CHAPTER 2. SITUATION ANALYSIS

This section of the plan concentrates on summarizing the conclusions you have drawn from Part 1 of the plan – the sales and market review – and starts with the SWOT analysis.

2.1 SWOT Analysis

Business class	B2C Products ✔	B2B Products ✔	B2C Services ✔	B2B Services ✔
Plan level	Basic ✔		Intermediate ✔	Advanced ✔

SWOT is an acronym for Strengths Weaknesses Opportunities and Threats. It is a method of analyzing the business and the external environment to decide what to stress, what to minimize, and how. It enables you to review both internal and external forces and draw together the conclusions you have determined from your research and analysis thus far.

Strengths and weaknesses concentrate on your internal characteristics.

Opportunities and threats arise from conditions external to your business. Naturally you only need to record the factors that have the most impact on your operations and which have the greatest immediacy.

Table 4 lists some of the influences you should consider in your SWOT.

The last six factors listed under 'Opportunities & Threats' are grouped under the acronym PESTLE to describe a framework for the following macro environmental factors:

Political – Tax policy, employment laws, environmental regulations, trade restrictions and tariffs and political stability.

Economic – Economic growth or decline, interest rates, exchange rates and inflation rates.

Social – Health consciousness, population growth rates, age distribution, career attitudes and safety emphasis.

Technological – R&D activity, automation, technology incentives and rate of technological exchange.

Legal – Changes in legislation that may affect the way in which you market your product or service.

Environment – public or government shifts in attitudes concerning the macro environment.

You need to be able to capitalize on your strengths and opportunities while defending or improving weaknesses and threats. Once recognized, every weakness presents a potential strength.

When you have identified your strengths and weaknesses and your opportunities and threats you can refine the implications of the SWOT analysis by summarizing:

- Key leverage points
- Business implications
- Sustainable competitive advantages

The format shown in Template 9 draws the threads of the analysis process together and allows you to crystallize your priorities.

Having identified your most important strategic decisions and set your priorities you can set your long-term goals and short-term objectives, which together form the foundation of your marketing plan.

Goals have to be measurable, have a deadline and be assigned as someone's specific responsibility. They must be believable and achievable.

Goals direct and control actions. They give you something to aim at and to measure progress. In order to achieve the goals, break them down into short and long term objectives.

TABLE 4 - SWOT analysis component examples

Strengths and Weaknesses (Internal influences)	Opportunities and Threats (External influences)
Profitability	Level of competition
Sales & marketing resources	Market growth and dynamics
Product quality	Presence or absence of brand loyalty
Financial management & resources	High or low barriers to entry
Production capability & capacity	Imports & exports dynamics
Distribution channels	Legal issues
People skills	Political factors
Reputation	Economic factors
Customer base and loyalty	Social factors
Strong brands	Technological factors
Research & development	Legal issues
Export capabilities	Environment factors

"Every weakness represents a potential strength"

Template 9 - SWOT analysis (example)

STRENGTHS (Internal)
1. Excellent product quality and design capability.
2. A growing understanding and appreciation of market dynamics.
3. Good liquidity and debt free as a result of sound financial management.
4. Ample production capacity.
5. A stable and skilled workforce.

WEAKNESSES (internal)
1. Static sales of existing products in a mature market.
2. No significant growth prospects on the horizon in existing product class.
3. Virtually no marketing programs in place at present.
4. Distribution limited to too few outlets making us vulnerable to deletion and diminishing market presence.

KEY LEVERAGE POINTS
We need to leverage our production and design strengths and harness our financial resources to establish a commanding presence in a growing market segment niche not yet universally identified by existing large competitors.

OPPORTUNITIES (external)
1. Strong growth in demand for furniture for small and home offices such as high end work stations.
2. These market segments are not dominated by existing suppliers.
3. Finance is available for expansion if needed.
4. Internet marketing offers potential.

THREATS (external)
1. Imports of standard office furniture products are growing.
2. Increasing competition as other small furniture manufacturers are constantly entering the office furniture segment.
3. Large and small end users are replacing conventional desks with more efficient workstations.

BUSINESS IMPLICATIONS
1. We need to be less vulnerable to imports and to target our market more effectively.
2. We also need to change our focus from a declining highly competitive market to one that is growing and is less vulnerable to competition.

SUSTAINABLE COMPETITIVE ADVANTAGES
We have the ability to capitalize on our established production strengths coupled with our acquired marketing orientation to recognize and target more potentially rewarding and less competitive new product market segments such as specialized work stations for small and home offices.

2.2 Mission Statement

Business class	B2C Products ✔	B2B Products ✔	B2C Services ✔	B2B Services ✔
Plan level	Basic ✘		Intermediate ✔	Advanced ✔

A mission statement is a 'big picture' reference point for the determination of future strategic decisions.

The first step is to define what business you are in.

This can be done in a variety of ways so you need to consider which is the most relevant for your product or service.

Business definitions describe broader long term parameters as opposed to self-limiting narrow definitions which may be changed by technology, social or fashion developments.

Vision is an important part of defining what business you are in.

TABLE 5 - Business definitions examples

Narrow product definition	Broad category definition
Carbonated beverages	Consumer refreshment
Desk top printers	Business communications equipment
Insurance	Asset protection
DVD Players	Home entertainment equipment
Paper and plastic bags	Domestic and industrial packaging
Popcorn and corn chips	Snack foods
Lawn mowing	Garden maintenance services
Domestic air conditioners and heaters	Home comfort

The next step is to write a mission statement. This is a statement of the business's reason for existence, what it wants to accomplish and be recognized for.

The mission statement makes it much simpler to select and evaluate appropriate long-term goals for your business.

Mission statements do not limit your scope but make day-to-day strategic decisions easier to make within a specific context.

The mission statement should include values and benefits to you, the community and employees – not just commercial goals.

A mission statement says what your company "stands for" in the marketplace and the broader community without being too patronizing.

Well-chosen and relevant words create a mental image that provides a sense of direction, a purpose and energy to what the enterprise does.

Once completed mission statements can be framed and placed in a prominent place as a reminder to employees and customers of what you as an organization stand for and what you are endeavoring to represent.

Template 10 - Mission statement components (example)	
Business we are in	State-of-the-art equipment for small and home offices
The products we produce	State of the art work station furniture
The customers we serve	People working from small offices/home offices and who are early adopters of developments in office technology
The area we serve	The city and surrounding districts of San Diego CA
The benefits to customers	Efficient, comfortable and flexible work station furniture that creates an environment for improved functionality and productivity
The benefits to the community	Being a responsible employer and supporter of local community affairs
The benefits to our employees	Fair compensation for effort in a secure, stable employment environment
The benefits to us	We seek a fair and reasonable return on investment over the long term.

MISSION STATEMENT EXAMPLE

Wellbuilt Office Furniture

OUR MISSION STATEMENT

Our corporate mission is to provide people working from small offices/home offices in San Diego and surrounding districts with the most efficient and comfortable office work equipment possible.

We further wish to create a secure stable employment environment in which our employees are fairly compensated for reliability, the manufacture of quality products and the provision of excellent customer service.

We seek fair and reasonable return on investment to keep the company financially healthy over the long term while taking our place as responsible employers and good corporate citizens.

"Mission statements free you from continually grappling with strategic decisions"

2.3 Target Markets

Business class	B2C Products ✔	B2B Products ✔	B2C Services ✔	B2B Services ✔
Plan level	Basic ✘	Intermediate ✔		Advanced ✔

Definition: *A target market is a tightly defined set of customers whose needs you intend to satisfy.*

You can break your market up further by defining target markets within market segments and sub segments. For example, you could refine customer profiles by age, gender, income groups, and other demographics.

One of the best ways to identify your target market is to look at your existing customer base. Who are your ideal clients? What do they have in common?

If you do not have an existing customer base, or if you are targeting a completely new audience, speculate on who they might be, based on their needs and the benefits they will receive. Investigate competitors or similar businesses in other markets to gain insights.

Target marketing is an ongoing process.

Who is most likely to buy from you? These people are at the center or bull's-eye of your target market. They can be defined by the following criteria:

1. Geographic profile: The location, size of the area, population, population density, and climate zone of your customers.

2. Demographic: The age, gender, income group, family composition, household type and size, occupation, and education of your customers.[1]

3. Psychographics: Personality type, behavior characteristics, life-style, rate of use, repetition of need, benefits sought, and loyalty characteristics of your customers.

4. Behavioral: The needs they seek to fulfill, the level of knowledge, information sources, attitudes, use or attitude to a product.

5. Business markets: Type (manufacturer, retail, wholesale, service), industry, size of business, financial strength, number of employees, location, structure, turnover and special requirements.

You could take this further by identifying the factors that influence them to buy particular specific products such as safety, comfort, prestige, performance, and other lifestyle considerations.

When you have done this, you have a clearer perspective as to how you can efficiently reach and appeal to these groups through personal selling, advertising or other forms of promotions and what kinds of messages are likely to strike a chord.

Target marketing can be compared with using a rifle (accurately targeted) as opposed to a shotgun (scatters over a wider area with extensive wastage).

Always aim as accurately as you can at the core of your target market for the most effective marketing results.

---

[1]. It can be beneficial to use 'Generation' definitions in defining target market demographics such as 'Baby Boomers' born between 1946 to 1964, Generation 'X' born between 1965 to 1977, Generation 'Y' (or Millennials) born between 1978 to 1994 and Generation 'Z' born since 1995.

Template 11 – Consumer target market characteristics (example)	
Product: Work station modules	Target market: Small office/home office
Geographics	
Location	San Diego and surrounding districts
Area size	50 square miles
Population	1,223,400
Population density	High
Climate zone	Temperate
Demographics	
Age range	25 -55 (Late Baby Boomers/Gen X & Y)
Gender split	60/40 Female/male
Income group	Medium to high
Family composition	Average 4 persons per household
Household type & size	Free standing units
Occupation	Professional
Education	College graduates
Psychographics	
Personality type	High achievers
Behavior characteristics	Strong work ethic, early adopters
Life style	Often combine work with raising families
Rate of use	Daily
Repetition of need	Constant
Benefits sought	Comfort, efficiency, flexibility
Loyalty characteristics	Strong loyalty when needs met
Behavioral	
Needs to be fulfilled	Career and business success
Knowledge level	High
Information sources	Internet
Attitudes	Self-starters
Use or response to a product	Expects and demands the highest quality

"Always aim at the core of your target market"

Template 12 – Business target markets characteristics (example)	
Product: Work station modules Target market: Small office/home office	
Business type (manufacturer, retail, wholesale, professional, service)	Professional & service
Industry	Various
Size of business	Small to medium
Financial strength	Sound
Number of employees	1 to 20
Location	San Diego and surrounding districts
Employment type	Self employed
Turnover	$100,000 to $500,000 pa
Special requirements	Time poor

2.4 Keys to Success

Business class	B2C Products ✔	B2B Products ✔	B2C Services ✔	B2B Services ✔
Plan level	Basic ✘	Intermediate ✔		Advanced ✔

This section of the plan consists of a summary of the components that you believe are essential for the plan to succeed. If they are not in place the fulfilment of the plan will be placed at risk.

Keys to success vary from one product and product category to another. For example a prerequisite for a florist may be volume of passing traffic, for an electrician or plumber it may be a 24 hour service, for a courier service it may be same day delivery.

The conclusions you draw are based on the primary market research you have conducted to date. If you do not have a good understanding of the keys to success you may need to research them further.

Examples include:
- A product or service with a meaningful competitive edge.
- An ability to charge a premium price
- A promotional program that reaches the right people at the right time with the right message
- Saturation distribution of the product in the selected geographical markets
- Gaining the support of the retail trade
- A interactive website that enables efficient e-commerce transactions
- Outstanding customer service
- An ability to retain existing clients.

When you have thought through the keys to success you can give additional attention to them to make sure they are in place and meet the required criteria.

Template 13 - Keys to success (example)

Product: ScHo Modular work stations

Keys to success	Comments
Meaningful competitive edge	The modular system is unique and meaningful.
Ability to charge a premium price	Advanced technical design with quality materials and workmanship will justify premium pricing.
An effective promotional program	We are confident that our carefully selected promotional program will be effective.
Saturation cistribution	We have identified the key retailers whose support is critical to the success of the venture.
Retail trade support	We have budgeted for an attractive retail margin and a comprehensive retail support program.
Interactive e-commerce website	Initially we will promote the e-commerce feature of the site in areas in which we do not have adequate retail distribution
Outstanding customer service	We have plans in place to provide both retail stockists and end users with exceptional customer service.

2.5 Critical Issues

Business class	B2C Products ✓	B2B Products ✓	B2C Services ✓	B2B Services ✓
Plan level	Basic ✗	Intermediate ✓		Advanced ✓

Critical issues are the assumptions you make in the plan which will cause the plan to fall short of the set objectives if they do not occur. They can be drawn from both internal and external influences and unlike keys to success critical issues may be beyond your direct control.

Examples include:
- The economy grows at a specified rate.
- You are able to secure the finance needed to execute the plan
- You are able to retain key employees
- The market will grow or at least remain constant
- No new directly head-to-head competitors enter the market
- You are able to identify channel partners that allow achievement of the distribution objectives
- Your supply source has the flexibility to meet demand
- No drastic changes to raw material prices and availability.

If you find that the critical issues do not eventuate as planned you will have to either rethink the issues or change those parts of the plan that are critically affected during the period of the plan's implementation.

Template 14 - Critical issues (example)

Product: SoHo Modular work stations

Critical Issues	Comments
The home offices/small offices growth trend is continuing and sustainable	Big business downsizing will maintain and hopefully accelerate the trend towards out-sourcing.
We do not meet any head-to-head competition in the first five years (including imports).	Major competitors do not seem to have yet recognized or focused on the small office/home office trend.
The retail trade supports stocking our product	We have a multi-tiered strategy to gain retail trade support. Initial indications are positive.
End users accept the modular concept	Preliminary marketing research indicates strong support for the concept.

Other: It is critical that we remain focused and do not fall into the trap of spreading our resources too thinly over too many budget items.

CHAPTER 3. MARKETING AND SALES OBJECTIVES
3.1 Marketing Objectives

Business class	B2C Products ✔	B2B Products ✔	B2C Services ✔	B2B Services ✔
Plan level	Basic ✔	Intermediate ✔		Advanced ✔

Before setting out to write your plan think carefully about what exactly you want to achieve for your products or services in the market overall. Remember these are marketing objectives and should not be confused with subordinate goals such as those for sales, profit or other targets.

Think of them as the primary opportunities you see to strategically grow your business.

They should arise from the findings and conclusions drawn from the market, sales, product and other reviews you have already completed and which were crystallized in your SWOT analysis.

The strategies you devise in the plan will flow from the primary objectives you set here at the outset.

Depending on your company's specific circumstances, typical objectives you could set could be increasing market share, expanding into new geographical markets or product segments, introducing new products, attracting new users, increasing your brand awareness or changing your brand image.

Marketing objectives should be easy to understand, quantifiable and set within given time frames so that progress against the objectives can be easily measured. They should be realistic and achievable while stretching your resources within reasonable limits.

The more specific your objectives are – the better.

They may very well change from one year to another as market dynamics change along with your individual position within it.

Most marketing objectives fall into four broad categories.

The framework shown indicates four common categories (which are by no means comprehensive) in which marketing objectives are developed and may help you to identify the objectives it would be sensible to consider and set in your particular circumstances.

TABLE 6. - Marketing objectives framework

	Existing Products	New Products
Existing markets	1. Market penetration	3. Product development
New markets	2. Market development	4. Diversification

1. **Market penetration:** Expanding penetration of existing markets with existing products.
2. **Market development**: Expanding into new markets with existing products.
3. **Product development**: Developing new products for existing markets.
4. **Diversification:** Developing new products for new markets.

Template 15 - Marketing objectives (example)

Product: Work station modules. Market segment: Small offices/home offices.

Marketing Objective	Time Frame	How Measured
10% share of office furniture purchases in small office and home office market segments	End year 1.	Retail trade data.
50% share of office furniture purchases in small office and home office market segments. Expand distribution into Los Angeles	End Year 2.	Retail trade data.
Establish awareness of and consumer demand for SoHo brand name	Progressively over the next three years	Telephone surveys among small office/home office proprietors
Expand distribution into Los Angeles	Year 4.	Achievement of set revenue and profit goals.
Expand distribution into San Francisco	Year 5.	As above

Marketing objectives define what you want to achieve in the *market overall*. They are the primary opportunities you see to strategically grow your business.

Marketing Objective Example: Our overall objective is new product development aimed at the existing and rapidly developing Small office/ Home Office market segment with an aim of establishing a 10% share of that market segment by the end of Year 1 and achieving a 50% market share by the end of Year 3 to give us the market leadership in the segment. This will be achieved by persuading existing and new small office/home office operators to replace conventional office desks with more efficient SoHo work station modules.

This will be followed by capitalizing on our initial success in our home market by expanding distribution into Los Angeles in year 4 and into San Francisco in year 5.

3.2 Sales Objectives

Business class	B2C Products ✔	B2B Products ✔	B2C Services ✔	B2B Services ✔
Plan level	Basic ✔	Intermediate ✔	Advanced ✔	

This is a summary of your products or services by individual product or product group, showing sales objectives (or actual sales) for the current year followed by the objectives for the first year of the plan along with forecasts for years 2 and 3 showing:
- Sales by value: Revenue received from sales
- Sales by volume: The number of products sold expressed in units

The schedule is based on the conclusions you have drawn and the strategies you intend to follow. It indicates where you will be directing your efforts in terms of investment and development.

The sales objectives should also be consistent with set marketing objectives such as market shares based on market size estimates.

What has occurred in the past is always the most logical starting point. It is always better to err on the conservative side with your estimates while remaining in keeping with the resources you have allocated.

You may need to constantly 'revisit' the goals you have set as market conditions improve or deteriorate. This may lead you to changing or fine-tuning some of the strategies you have previously developed.

Remember the plan is a flexible changing document with each part interactive with all or some of the others. At the first draft you may find that the calculations you have entered do not make financial sense or that you do not have the production capacity to meet the plan or some other aspect that is anomalous to what you are endeavoring to achieve. If this is the case re-work some or all of the objectives until they align and are completely practical.

Template 16 - Sales objectives – existing & new products (example)

Product (or product group): Office furniture

Existing Products	Current Year		Year 1 of plan		Year 2 Forecast		Year 3 Forecast	
	# of units	$000's	# of units	$000's	# of units	$000's	# of units	$000's
Desks	1,000	700	1,000	700	900	630	800	560
Returns	500	200	500	200	430	180	380	160
Screens	200	100	200	100	180	90	170	85
Total existing products	1,700	1,000	1,700	1,000	1,510	900	1350	805
New Products (Work stations)	0	0	500	300	1,000	600	1,825	1095
TOTAL ALL PRODUCTS	1,700	1,000	2,200	1,300	2,510	1,500	3,175	1,900

CHAPTER 4. MARKETING STRATEGIES

"Marketing strategy is a series of integrated actions leading to sustainable competitive advantage". - John Scully

This chapter sets out how you are going to achieve your goals. It includes which elements of the marketing mix you have selected to achieve your marketing, sales and profit objectives. Marketing strategies can be broadly classified as "above the line" or "below the line".

"Above the line" (also known as 'theme') relates to media advertising such as advertising placed in newspapers, magazines, TV, radio, outdoor or transportation, and any internet advertising. "Below the line"(also known as 'scheme') refers to all other promotional activities such as price oriented special offers as "two for the price of one", deals and allowances in which consumers are offered discounted prices for a limited period, point-of-sale advertising materials, consumer promotions such as competitions and contests, retail promotions in which floor space is negotiated for special displays, and direct (or database) marketing.

As a rule of thumb fast moving consumer goods (FMCG) marketing budgets are often allocated 50/50 above the line/below the line. Industrial and business-to-business products (B2B) and services may allocate the split more heavily to "below the line activities – possibly as much as 10/90 above/below the line.

Just as a conductor directs an orchestra, part of the secret of a successful marketing plan is to orchestrate each of the components of the plan so that they complement the others synergistically. For example, pricing, advertising, sales promotion and packaging should all be contributing to the same statement about your product or service. Strategies can be broken down into one of four categories known as the 4 P's of marketing which constitute "the marketing mix". [1]

The 4 Ps of Marketing

The 4 Ps of marketing are Product, Place, Price, and Promotion. Think of each of these as variables over which you have complete control. The idea is to set these variables in such a way that sales will occur.

---

1. In the 1960's Professor Neil Borden of the Harvard Business School named the actions that can influence the sale of goods and services 'the marketing mix'. At around the same time Professor E. Jerome McCarthy, also of the Harvard Business School, suggested the marketing mix contained four components: product, price, promotion and place. Some marketing practitioners add a fifth P to the mix – Profit - on the basis that if you are pouring money into marketing and nothing is happening you need to re-evaluate your marketing mix.

You cannot "compel" a customer to purchase, but you can certainly influence his or her decision by setting the "right" price, making it available at a convenient retail location, make the style of advertising and promotion appealing and visible, while designing the product in such way that it meets a particular purpose. You control the entire process in such a way that it will influence the consumer to purchase – but only if it fills a 'need' or 'want'.

These variables are all interdependent but when combined together they form 'the right mix'. This is often referred to as the marketing mix. In creating the mix you need to consider all prevailing external influences such as the competition, current fashions, changing technology and environmental factors.

The aim is to arrive at a mix that will clearly differentiate your products from those of your competitors while achieving your corporate goals. For example, your company may wish to offer a premium priced luxury product when your competitors are appealing to the mass market. This should be consistent with the business definition, objectives and mission statement you have previously defined.

PRODUCT

When analyzing your products or services you need to understand what it is that you are really offering the purchaser. Is it the physical object or what the object represents? Is it tangible or intangible? What needs does it fill? Are they physical or psychological? What are the underlying needs or wants?

People often buy prestige brands not because the product is more functional than the competition but because it makes a positive statement about the owner.

Regardless of the buying motive it is the product that is ultimately transacted. In order to maximize sales potential you need to understand exactly what it is that motivates a buyer to purchase. When you have a sound appreciation of this you will know how to promote and position the product and what senses to appeal to.

4.1.1 Product (or Service) Development

Business class	B2C Products ✔	B2B Products ✔	B2C Services ✔	B2B Services ✔
Plan level	Basic ✔	Intermediate ✔		Advanced ✔

Product development involves the translation of product concepts to actual products in the marketplace that meet consumers' needs and wants.

New products are the lifeblood of any business. New products help you to stay one step ahead of your competitors. Without a constant stream of new products your business will eventually come to a standstill. Every business, by definition, has an obligation to be permanently active in developing new products and services and in seeking out new product development opportunities.

New product ideas are gleaned from many sources. Your customers, competitors, overseas markets, trade magazines, market research programs, and the internet, are excellent places to start and should be constantly monitored.

TABLE 7. The Four Ps of the Marketing Mix

The Marketing Mix

Product
- Development
- Proposition
- Positioning
- Quality
- Features
- Options
- Styles
- Range
- Branding
- Brand image
- Packaging
- Sizes
- Warranties
- Servicing
- Research

Place
- Channels
- Locations
- Inventory
- Transport
- Agents
- Distributors
- Export
- Supply chain management

Price
- Pricing strategies
- Pricing tactics
- List price
- Discounts
- Allowances
- Payment period
- Credit terms
- Consignment terms
- Deals
- Refund policy
- Bundling

Promotion
- Sales management
- New business prospecting
- Customer service
- Advertising
- Sales promotion
- Online marketing
- Merchandising
- Publicity & PR
- Corporate communications
- Direct & database marketing
- Social media
- Trade shows
- Sponsorship

Apple famously seem to have the knack of recognizing consumer needs or wants before consumers themselves actually do.

Before investing in a new product you cannot be too diligent about researching the market to ensure the product concept is what people want or need.

The concept may start with your ideas and theories but these must be tested against your potential customers' reactions. Remember it is not what you want but what your customers and potential customers want.

Every year companies around the world spend billions launching new products. The odds are stacked against them: Upwards of 70 per cent of new products fail in the first 18 months. Many more do not meet initial expectations and soon become non-viable because they do not meet consumer needs or wants.

You cannot take the risk out of new product development but you can reduce the risk considerably with astute planning and quality market and marketing research.

Template 17 - Product development checklist (example)

Criteria checklist	Responses
What is the product concept?	High tech/high quality work stations
What are its features?	Compact integration of computers and peripherals
What are its benefits?	Improved functionality and efficiency
What is the proposed target market	Small offices and home offices
Will this product replace an existing product or create a new product segment?	Replaces conventional desks and other office furniture
Can it be produced with our existing facilities?	Yes with minor modifications
What pricing strategy is envisaged?	Premium price to fit premium quality strategy
How will it be branded?	Under the 'Soho" brand
How will it be distributed?	Via office supply chains and general furniture retailers
How will it be packaged?	In ready to assemble flat pack kits
How will it be communicated to the target market?	Media advertising, trade shows, in-store displays retailers cooperative ads and catalogues
Which products will it compete against?	Conventional office desks and tables
What market research is proposed?	Focus groups among target market
What is the market research budget	$10,000
What is the product development budget?	$30,000
What is the proposed marketing budget?	$480,000
What are the perceived risks?	Time it takes and cost of getting the message across to a critical mass of customers
What is the proposed launch date?	February 2018

Template 18 - Product development schedule (example)

Product development stage	Target completion date	Responsibility
Production of prototype or sample	Mid 2017	Dennis/Mark
Marketing & trade research	September 2017	Mark
Finalize packaging design	October 2017	Dennis
Commence commercial production	January 2018	Mark
Trade launch date	February 2018	Mark
Commence distribution	March 2018	Mark
Consumer launch date	April 2018	Mark
Post launch evaluation	June 2018	Mark/Dennis

4.1.2 Product Proposition

Business class	B2C Products ✔	B2B Products ✔	B2C Services ✔	B2B Services ✔
Plan level	Basic ✔	Intermediate ✔		Advanced ✔

Definition: *A product proposition is an offer to your customers or prospects that give them a compelling reason to do business with you instead of your competitors.*

This may also be referred to as the 'remarkable difference'.

The noted copywriter Rosser Reeves from the famous Ted Bates agency coined the term *unique selling proposition* or USP as far back as the 1940's.

He defined a Unique Selling Proposition as an offer which has unique benefits, which the competition cannot or does not offer. It is a proposition so strong that it pulls new customers to your product. It is as valid today as it was way back then.

Once identified and efficiently communicated a product proposition can give your product a permanent competitive edge and become an invaluable marketing asset.

'Getting in first' is critical to the establishment of a product proposition. The one that establishes itself first is the hardest to dislodge.

A product proposition can be tangible as in a product feature or attribute or intangible such as in a lifestyle or image association. Very often it is not about functionality but what it is that the product or brand says about you.

A product proposition gives a product or service a raison d'être – a reason for being or the purpose of its existence – why you should buy 'x' instead of 'y'.

A product proposition separates your product or service from the competition

They are often expressed as slogans, catch phrases or theme lines as in the following examples.

PRODUCT PROPOSITION EXAMPLES

"A glass and a half of full cream milk in every block of Cadbury's chocolate"
"Only Schweppes has Schweppervescence"
"You'll be lovelier every day with fabulous Pink Camay"
"You'll wonder where the yellow went when you brush your teeth with Pepsodent"
"If it saves your life once a year — it's a Goodyear"
"A Mars a day helps you work, rest and play"
"Guinness is good for you"
"When it absolutely, positively has to be there overnight" (Federal Express)
"Dominos Pizza — delivered in 30 minutes or it's free"
Joe's Plumbing Services — on tap day and night"
"The flame grilled burgers are better at Hungry Jacks"
"Solo Lemon — Light on the fizz so you can slam it down fast"

"A product proposition gives a product 'a reason for being"

Think about your product or service and consider what makes it better than the others in the field. What do people look for in products like yours? Depending on the product category:

a) Does your product offer better quality?
b) Does it have unique ingredients or materials?
c) Is it more efficient or functional?
d) Does it offer better value?
e) Does it make an appealing promise?
f) Does it taste better?
g) Is it healthier?
h) Does it last longer…or
i) Does it have an attribute of particular appeal to the category?

Jot down your thoughts as they arise. Then narrow it down to the one that offers the most promise and refine the proposition to a short catchy line that you can use in all forms of your advertising and corporate communications.

There is an old saying in marketing: "Sell the sizzle, not the steak". This means it is better to sell the benefits the products offers to the purchaser – not the features of or the quality of the product itself. It answers the question, "What's in it for me". After all that is what the consumer is really interested in.

"Each strategy should be complementary and synergistic"

Template 19 - Product proposition development (example)

Product: SoHo work station modules

Product Proposition Options	Proposition Expression	Scale of appeal Rating 1-10
Efficiency and functionality	Higher productivity in less work space	10
Sit or stand functionality	Adjustable desk top provides healthy circulation and movement options	8
Product design	Modular office furniture functionality for computerized offices	7
Product quality	The modules will be produced in a range of high-end scratch resistant finishes and colors.	5

Preferred primary product proposition expression: "SoHo work stations deliver higher productivity in less floor space".

4.1.3 Positioning

Business class	B2C Products ✔	B2B Products ✔	B2C Services ✔	B2B Services ✔
Plan level	Basic ✘	Intermediate ✔		Advanced ✔

Definition: *Positioning is identifying a real or perceived gap in the market that is not being filled.*

A unique market position allows you to create a clear niche in the consumers mind. It is what differentiates your product, brand or organization from your competitors and reduces direct head-to-head competition in a crowded market. Positioning can be either tangible or intangible.

Positioning is one of the most important aspects of a brand strategy and arguably the least understood. It is one of the most valuable skill in a marketer's armory. Once a brand has achieved a strong position, it can be difficult to dislodge. Positioning can be about what a product does or who it is for, it can be about usage occasions, pricing, intention for a particular target market or an aspirational lifestyle or its place in the market relative to the market leader among many other variables.

Positioning maps

The positioning map is a useful tool to help you identify a commercially viable market position and to compare the perceived or real difference between your competitors' positioning with your own. The device enables you to determine if there are any commercially viable 'gaps' in the market you could fill.

Each positioning map has an axis for two sets of variables (such as price and quality). The variables selected will vary from one product category to another and are chosen according to the most important criteria for each.

You can plot the position of each competitor as shown in the positioning map example below.

When the map is completed you may find that many competitors are clustered in close proximity meaning that they are competing directly with each other. This leaves the potential to adopt a different position with less direct competition. Before adopting a particular position research the market thoroughly to make sure that the position you are planning to occupy is commercially viable.

Positioning maps can be based on any number of parameters. For example a product may be:

a) Targeted to a particular group of people.
b) Intended to be used in a certain way
c) Intended to be used or consumed at a certain time or occasion
d) Occupying a particular price point (high or low).
e) An unusual point of difference

Positioning Map Example
Product: Office work stations

	High price/high quality	
Large corporate offices	● Manufacturer A ● Manufacturer B	Unoccupied segment representing opportunity for Wellbuilt
	● Manufacturer C	● Manufacturer D
	Low price/low quality	

(Left axis label: Large corporate offices; Right axis label: Small offices/home offices)

In the example above, there are two major office furniture manufacturers competing in the large corporate office/high price segment (A & B), one manufacturer in the large corporate office/low price segment (C) and one in the small office/home office/low price segment (D). There are currently no manufacturers in the fast growing small office/home office high price/high quality segment thus presenting a potential 'market gap' opportunity.

Positioning maps rely on the demand of the variables plotted as determined by informed analysis and market research. There are almost as many variables as there are product categories. Price is usually one of the variables in a positioning map but end user demographics, usage occasions, product characteristics, seasonality etc. are also common in determining more precise positions.

Examples of positioning map variables:
Price and quality (e.g. consumer durables)
Price and service (e.g. tradesmen, accountants, all other service providers)
Usage occasions (e.g. food and beverages)
User group by gender and age group (e.g. video games)
Store environment and product range (e.g. bookshop)
Quality and functionality (e.g. machinery)

Positioning statements
If you identify a unique position for your product or service try to craft a few well-chosen words in to a positioning statement and use it in your advertising, packaging, stationery, corporate brochures, website, staff uniforms and everywhere else your product or service is promoted.

This will help to communicate your position to potential customers and to crystallize it in their minds.

Like product propositions, (to which they are closelely allied), compelling and unique positioning statements are not easy to identify (which makes them all the more valuable when you do).

POSITIONING STATEMENT EXAMPLES

"Over 50's Insurance Agency"
Woolworths — The fresh food people"
"Avis — #2 in rent-a-cars"
"7-Up — The Uncola"
"Coke — It's the real thing"
(Introduced in 1969 and possible the best Coca Cola positioning ever for recall)
"BMW — The ultimate driving machine"
"Fisherman's Friend throat lozenges — The strongest there is"
"Sleeptite cough drops — help you sleep through the night"
"Bounty chocolate bars — The quicker picker upper"
"Solo Lemon — A man's drink"

Positioning differentiates your products or services from your competitors

Template 20 - Product positioning statement development (example)

Product: SoHo work station modules

Positioning options checklist	Positioning statement	Scale of uniqueness rating 1 to 10
User group	For the small Office/Home Office".	10
Product quality and functionality	The ultimate in high tech quality and functionality	10
Price and quality	At the premium end of the price scale	10
Price & service	Not applicable in this example	0
Usage occasions	Not applicable in this example	0
Store environment and product range	Not applicable in this example	0

Preferred positioning statement: "The ultimate in modular high tech/functional work stations for state-of-the-art Small Offices/Home Offices".

4.1.4 Branding

Business class	B2C Products ✔	B2B Products ✔	B2C Services ✔	B2B Services ✔
Plan level	Basic ✔		Intermediate ✔	Advanced ✔

Strong branding is another factor that is crucial to success in the market.

Brands are a company's most treasured assets. You cannot place a monetary value on a well-known, respected brand name.

If you are not marketing a brand you are merely selling a commodity leaving yourself vulnerable to the whims and vagaries of a price sensitive market.

Consumers are willing to pay a premium for trusted brand names. This is known as 'brand equity'. Brand equity describes the value of a strong brand name based on the notion that the owner of the brand can generate more sales and profits from that brand than products with a less well established and trusted brand.

Imagine trying to put a value on brands like Apple, Google, Coca Cola, Microsoft, Toyota, IBM, Samsung, Amazon, Mercedes Benz, General Electric, BMW, McDonalds, Disney, Intel, Facebook, Cisco, Oracle, Nike, Louis Vuitton and H&M. These brands have the ability to command higher sales and profits compared with lesser known competitive brands. (They topped the list of the world's 100 most valuable brands in 2016 as measured by *Interbrand*).

Companies that have developed brand names that become household words have created priceless goodwill.

Brands have become the spoils of takeover wars. We often hear "we bought that company because of its brands". Brands become entities only after years – even decades of sustained strategic investment.

Supermarkets and showrooms are full of commodities but consumers look for and buy brands.

Established brands are like trusted friends. You can rely upon them, you are familiar with them - and they never let you down. They create consumer loyalty.

Strong brands are the common denominator of successful enterprises. People come and go but great brands are timeless.

It is time and money well spent in researching, defining, and building your brand. Your brand is a promise to your customers. It is a key part of successful marketing.

Devising a distinctive brand name and identifying one that is legally available for use, is a challenge in itself. Before you can use a brand name it must first be accepted by the Trade Marks' registrar (or the local equivalent in your country) as meeting all the legal requirements needed for registration.

Original brand names take years of investment and development before they are meaningful. For most SME's with limited resources it is impractical to attempt to build a 'stable' of brands each with its own personality.

A more practical course is to concentrate on building the business name as the corporate brand such as *Jim's Lawn Mowing* or *Mr. Fixit Computer Repairs*.

If you are a sole proprietor, using your own name in the business name has its advantages while also including the business category in the corporate name provides an immediate identification and positioning of the business you are in.

Price Brands

Some businesses use dual brand strategies to compete in both ends of the price market. This provides the opportunity to maintain the positioning and integrity of the premium brand while also competing in the low price end of the market with a cheap 'no frills' brand. Many manufacturers use this strategy to protect premium brands when price wars break out in the category.

"Any damn fool can put on a deal, but it takes genius, faith and perseverance to create a brand". David Ogilvy

Template 21 - Brand selection checklist (example)
Product: SoHo work station modules
Q. Is our corporate brand name widely recognized in the market in which we compete? ☒ Yes ☐ No
Q. If 'yes' would the addition of a description of the product or service category to the corporate name add to business identity and positioning? ☐ Yes ☐ No. Not applicable in this instance.
Q. Would the introduction of an original brand name offer marketing advantages? ☒ **Yes** ☐ **No**
Q. If 'yes' what are they? Describes and positions the product concept
Q. What branding strategy do our main competitors use? ☒ Corporate ☒ Original
Q. Are competitors' branding strategies more effective than ours? ☐ Yes ☒ No (At least not at present).
Q. Do we have access to potential brand names that could be developed? ☒ Yes ☐ No
Q. Are we prepared to invest resources required in the development of an original brand? ☒ Yes ☐ No
Q. Is there potential in the market for the introduction of a 'price' brand in addition to our established brand? ☐ Yes ☒ No At least not in the foreseeable future
Summary: We intend to market our product under the brand name 'SoHo' because it meets the criteria we are looking for.

4.1.5 Brand & Corporate Image

Business class	B2C Products ✓	B2B Products ✓	B2C Services ✓	B2B Services ✓
Plan level	Basic ✓		Intermediate ✓	Advanced ✓

Brand Image

Everything you do for a brand above and below the line contributes to the brand image. Just as individuals project very specific image attributes, so do brands and companies.

The brand image (or brand personality) is the set of beliefs that a person or group holds about a brand such as sophistication, wealth, discernment and other associations with actual or perceived users of that brand.

Marketers often use celebrities in advertising who represent the attributes of the desired brand image. The celebrities' images are reflected in the brand images by association.

Well defined brand images are important assets as consumers connect with image associations at a sub-conscious level as well as product attributes. Brands such as Rolex, Apple and Mercedes Benz are examples of this.

Positive brand images can command a premium over competitive brands with less well defined images. They are inherent qualities and are built over time as a result of consistent advertising and promotion in which the desired brand attributes are presented and portrayed.

Brand images are determined in 'top of mind' focus group discussions in which word association techniques are used. The key to brand image development is to establish the images a brand already has so that they can be further developed and reinforced in future brand communications.

A distinctive 'logo' (logotype) is an essential part of brand identity. A logo is a visual device that displays the brand name in a distinctive stylized typeface which can reflect and add to the desired brand image.

Corporate Image

Just as brand image is the set of beliefs individuals or groups hold about brands, the corporate image is the set of beliefs held about a company. It is a generally accepted image of what a company 'stands for'.

Corporate image is in a tier above the brands the company markets unless the corporate name is also the brand name such as you find with accountants, insurance brokers, solicitors, stock brokers, and so on.

It is equally important to invest in the development of the corporate image or company personality as it is with the brand image.

It is good marketing practice to define the adjectives you would like to describe the company or its brands to galvanize where you are and where you want to be. Adjectives such as reliable, dependable, friendly, innovative, hi-tech, stable etc. help you to define the image you wish to project.

Corporate image can be reinforced in company communications such as advertising, stationery, web presence, employee uniforms, signage and other aspects of corporate presentation.

Additional activities such as public relations and publicity, community involvement and sponsorships can further contribute to a positive corporate image.

Template 22 - Brand (or corporate) image checklist (example)

Q. What do we know about our current brand (or corporate) image among customers, prospects, suppliers and others in contact with the company?
A. Our company name is not established with the general public. We are therefore intending to establish a more descriptive and distinctive name for the proposed new product concept
Q. What do we want the brand image to be?
A. Technologically advanced, premium quality, state-of-the-art.
Q. If our brand was a person, what images attributes would we want to convey?
A. Solid, reliable, young, dynamic, dependable, clever, entrepreneurial, innovative, early adopter.
Q. How does our image compare with our nearest competitors?
A. As yet there are no significant competitors in the product segment we intend to enter
Q. How well does our current visual corporate identity contribute towards the desired brand image?
A. We will develop a new visual corporate identity in keeping with the desired brand image
Q. What steps can we take to strengthen the desired brand image among our customers, prospects, employees, suppliers and others?
A. We will portray the desired attributes in our website, advertising, promotions, packaging, pricing and social media and in all other corporate communications.

4.1.6 Packaging

Business class	B2C Products ✔	B2B Products ✔	B2C Services ✗	B2B Services ✗
Plan level	Basic ✔	Intermediate ✔		Advanced ✔

Packaging fills two important roles. The first is to provide functionality in terms of protecting the product contents. The second is a merchandising/display role at the point-of-sale.

In the functional role, packaging has to protect its contents and keep them in perfect order for the purchaser. For example cookie packaging must retain crispness and freshness. Soda bottles and cans must retain peak carbonation. Frozen ready to eat meals requires packaging that is microwave friendly. White goods packaging must protect the contents from dents and scratches.

'Tamperproof' packaging has also become a prerequisite in consumable products to protect consumers and manufacturers from malicious damage. And of course no packaging would be complete without those ubiquitous bar codes.

In the merchandising/display role the importance of this function cannot be over emphasized in today's crowded marketplace.

Some fast moving goods marketers believe that money spent on packaging and packaging design can be more effective than money spent on media advertising or merchandising materials.

Unlike media advertising, packaging is not remote from the product but is an integral part of it. Packaging graphics encompassing the use of color, design, display of your logo, sales propositions and usage instructions are all vital considerations and funds deployed is usually money well spent.

You can go a long way towards developing an entire brand image and personality through packaging alone.

Superior packaging can give a product a competitive advantage as effective as a product advantage.

Consistency of design and colour is important in long standing successful products. People become familiar with packaging. Radical changes might make consumers think the product is no longer available prompting a switch to another brand.

Products can have multiple packaging components. This may include the primary pack such as a bottle, can or carton, which may be enclosed in an 'outer' such as a cardboard box. Shipping cartons are also usually involved which contain multiple units. Each of these packages present communication opportunities to sway the end user at different stages of the sales process.

Template 23 - Packaging checklist (example)		
Criteria	Functionality	Graphics
What are the pros and cons of our packaging materials?	Our proposed packaging will be in well-designed 'flat packs' for economy in storage and transportation.	Eye catching graphics will illustrate the product concept, highlight the brand name and help to merchandise the product at the retail level.
What are the pros and cons of our main competitors packaging materials?	Not direct competitors at this stage	Not yet applicable.
What can we do to improve our packaging's functionality and design graphics	We will constantly monitor improvement opportunities and seek the advice of packaging suppliers.	We will study Ikeas approach to flat pack packaging and graphics as they are the leaders in the category.

PRICE

Price is the second 'P' of the marketing mix. It can - and should be every bit as creative as all other strategies in the plan. Devising price strategies and tactics is multifaceted and takes in a number of related considerations that influence how much end users pay for a product or service and what part of the revenue goes to the bottom line. Pricing is a crucial marketing consideration and has long since ceased to be the sole domain of accountants and financial controllers.

Pricing is one element of the marketing mix in which it is relatively easy to experiment. It is fairly simple to gauge the results of price adjustments by testing them on a small scale in pockets of the market in which all other elements are left constant.

Price setting

Here are the main factors you should consider when setting your price strategies and tactics.

Brand image and product positioning

Does the positioning and brand image of your product or service support selling at a discount, at parity or at a premium to your main competitors?

A high end positioning will normally be reflected in premium pricing while a 'price' or commodity brand will be sold at the lower end of the market with other positions falling somewhere in between. Are you aiming at the high volume/low pricing end or are you seeking low volume/high pricing?

It should be remembered that consumers usually weigh up cost in the context of value for money. Cost is usually equated with quality so the lowest price is not the sole consideration in purchasing decisions.

Distribution chain margins

When devising price points in the manufacturer to consumer distribution chain you need to consider acceptable margins for intermediaries at every step along the way.

An agent, wholesaler, distributor or retailer may not want to stock or 'push' your product if it does not meet acceptable industry norms or individual needs.

The competition

The process of setting price points begins with a review of your pricing relative to the competition. Is your current (or intended pricing) lower, higher or the same as the main competition? You then need to consider where you want to be.

Price sensitivity (elasticity)

Price elasticity in a particular market can determine the extent to which you have room to move. In some instances a small price rise may result in a collapse in sales. This is 'price inelasticity'. On the other hand price elasticity is when a large price rise results in only a small drop in sales.

As previously mentioned it is good practice to constantly test and monitor price elasticity ranges on a small controlled scale.

TABLE 8 - Factors that influence pricing
Primary
Brand image & product positioning
Distribution chain margins
Competition
Price sensitivity (elasticity)
Secondary
Cost of production & distribution
Required return on investment & profit margins
Perceived value to consumer
Product quality
Service
Location
Marketing strategies
Business overheads

"The real issue is value, not price". Robert T. Lindgren

4.2.1 Price Strategies

Business class	B2C Products ✔	B2B Products ✔	B2C Services ✔	B2B Services ✔
Plan level	Basic ✔		Intermediate ✔	Advanced ✔

Cost plus

In practice there are a number of price setting methods in place. One such method is known as 'cost plus'. After adding up all the fixed and variable costs in getting a product or service to market a fixed markup is added. For example a paint store proprietor might take the wholesale price of a can of paint, add an amount that covers store rental, staffing, utilities and other costs then add a further percentage markup. He can pursue this strategy as long as it does not make the retail price uncompetitive.

Market skimming

Another option to consider is to adopt a strategy of 'market skimming' or 'what the market will bear'. This can be done for the period in which demand is high and 'price elastic' such as when an item of new technology (such as a new Apple iPhone) is introduced ahead of the market. The advantage of price skimming is that it can compensate for high development costs. It can only be followed for the time it takes for competition to catch up.

Market penetration

This is the reverse of market skimming. Customers are attracted through low initial prices so that the price can be gradually increased when a viable market share has been acquired.

Loss leader

This entails selling a particular product at a narrow margin or even a small loss in order to attract customers into a store who will buy other more profitable products.

Premium pricing

The ability to command pricing at the upper end of the category yields huge marketing advantages. It allows the manufacturer the ability to spend more on marketing and promotion while taking a larger slice of sales revenue to the bottom line.

It also gives you the ability to be more flexible in passing on temporary price reductions, promotional allowances and quantity discounts.

Human nature being what it is means that people usually associate premium pricing with premium quality. This is why marketers should not be overly cautious with premium pricing because the fear that customers will not recognize value for money is often exaggerated.

It is sobering to consider that if you underprice your products by say 10 per cent, you will lose $1,000 in revenue for every $10,000 in turnover. It makes good sense to conduct a series of 'what if' analyses in which you factor in and compare different price and turnover projections.

Pricing is a crucial marketing function and has long since ceased to be the sole domain of accountants and financial controllers

Parity pricing

Some marketers elect to follow a policy of pricing at the same level as the mainstream market. They then seek to develop other competitive advantages, such as better products or service, better packaging or wider distribution.

Commodity pricing

Commodity pricing is when goods or services are offered at rock bottom prices on a 'no frills' basis. An example of this is an orchardist who sells fruit by the crate from a roadside stall.

This trading method does not present the opportunity to fund any serious marketing and relies on the premise of high volume/ low margin.

Captive pricing

This is the strategy of selling a primary product at a low price in order to capture customers who are obliged to purchase secondary products at premium prices. Common examples are computer inkjet and laser printers sold at rock bottom prices so that consumers purchase consumables such as ink and toner cartridges at inflated prices.

Template 24 - Competitive pricing analysis (example)

Product	List price $	End user price $	Retail Mark up	Retail Markup %	Retail Gross Margin %
Our product	$600 per module	$900 per module	$300	50%	33%
Competitor 1: Premier	$500	$700	$200	40%	29%
Competitor 2: Stylecraft	$450	$650	$200	44%	31%
Competitor 3: Colonial	$400	$600	$200	50%	33%

Template 25 - Pricing strategies (example)

The pricing strategies we intend to adopt are:

☐ Cost plus	☐ Market skimming	☐ Market penetration	☐ Loss Leader
☑ Premium pricing	☐ Parity pricing	☐ Commodity pricing	☐ Captive pricing

The rationale for adopting this options is: We have a quality product with little or no direct competition. Premium pricing will allow us to fund marketing and trade support. Our research indicated potential users are prepared to pay around $900 per module given the benefits they provide.

"The ability to command a premium price is an enormous competitive advantage"

4.2.2 Price Tactics

Business class	B2C Products ✔	B2B Products ✔	B2C Services ✔	B2B Services ✔
Plan level	Basic ✔	Intermediate ✔		Advanced ✔

Within the setting of pricing strategies there is an almost endless range of pricing tactics options that play a significant role in influencing market penetration. It is often good practice to set a high 'list price' while using pricing tactics beneath this to meet competitors' pricing or to gain your own short term price advantages.

Examples of pricing tactics include:

Short term discounts
These are often used to clear out old stock or to introduce a customer to a product to give them 'an opportunity to try' in the theory they will like the product enough to continue purchasing when pricing is restored to the normal level.

Quantity discounts
These can also be used to encourage large orders or to encourage multiple orders such as a soda company that offers price breaks based on the number of cases purchased, for example a 10 per cent discount off the list price could be offered on purchases of 100 cases or more.

Promotional allowances
These may be offered to a retailer for passing on to end users in conjunction with special in-store displays and the like.

Special payment or credit terms
These can take the form of extended terms of payment such as 'buy today – nothing to pay for 12 months'. This practice is common with 'big ticket' items such as furniture, electrical appliances, cars and computers.

Consignment terms
Under this arrangement, products are supplied to wholesalers or retailers without charge until sold. This encourages listings (carrying inventories) and provides an incentive to the intermediary to 'push' sales.

Refund policy
A refund policy gives purchasers 'consumer confidence' in the knowledge that they get their 'money fully refundable if not completely satisfied'.

Bundling
This is the tactic of combining two or more products and selling the 'bundle' for less than the cost of the products sold separately. This is a common tactic in the marketing of computer software and hardware and in fast food retailing such as a free Coke with every family size meal. Telcos may also bundle broadband and landline phone rental as another example.

"If you compete on price alone, all you are doing is supplying a commodity"

Template 26 - Price tactics (example)

The pricing tactics we intend to adopt are:			
☑ Short term discounts	☑ Quantity discounts	☑ Promotional allowances	
☑ Special payment or credit terms	☐ Consignment terms	☐ Refund policy	☐ Bundling
The rationale for adopting these options is: A 5% discount on quantities of 25 units or more will encourage maintenance of adequate stock levels while a further 5% discount will be paid for on-floor displays and temporary price reductions tied in with retailers' catalogue sales. We are also prepared to provide credit terms of 30 days from invoice. These tactics will be monitored on an ongoing basis and adjusted as deemed appropriate.			

PLACE

Place is that part of the marketing mix that is concerned with the 'place' where buyer and seller come together whether that be online, in a retail store, a service provider's direct interface with a customer or a manufacturer's showroom.

Place or 'placement' is closely linked with 'distribution' or the various channels you use to reach the end user.

Determining the most advantageous distribution channel (or channels) is a key part of the decision making process that requires careful research and planning.

If your products are not easily accessible to potential buyers they will purchase competitors' products that are more easily reached.

4.3.1 Business Location

Business class	B2C Products ✓	B2B Products ✓	B2C Services ✓	B2B Services ✓
Plan level	Basic ✓	Intermediate ✓	Advanced ✓	

The 'place' of business location is critical in the case of retail businesses and service providers that rely on local or passing trade (such as hairdressers, accountants, solicitors, medical clinics and other professional services).

If location is important, you need to evaluate:
- Passing pedestrian and traffic flow,
- Direct competition in the immediate area,
- Complementary businesses in the immediate area,
- Parking facilities,
- Rent costs and
- Location in relation to residential or commercial zones from which potential customers are drawn.

Template 27 - Business location analysis (example)

To what extent does the site affect your business	Not a great deal as the site is not a retail outlet but we intend to upgrade and make more extensive use of the showroom.
What is the rate of passing traffic?	Extensive
Is the site rental high, low or average?	Not applicable. We own the site.
Is passing traffic commensurate with rent?	Not applicable
Is the building in keeping with your desired image?	Not at present but we intend to upgrade
What is the extent of direct competition?	None
Are there complementary businesses in your area?	No.
Is customer parking adequate?	Yes.
Is there enough space for your operations?	Yes for the expected future.
Are there signage opportunities to attract customers?	Yes.
Is the site close to residential or commercial zones from which your customer base is drawn?	Yes
Is the location developing, reaching maturity or in decline?	Reaching maturity
Should we consider moving to a better location?	Not in the foreseeable future.

"Business location can make a critical difference in businesses that rely on local trade "

4.3.2 Distribution

Business class	B2C Products ✔	B2B Products ✔	B2C Services X	B2B Services X
Plan level	Basic ✔	Intermediate ✔		Advanced ✔

Mass distribution of your products is essential in the case of manufactured products that do not rely on local trade but have a much wider state or national distribution network.

There are often many options or distribution channels a product can take in going from your factory or warehouse to the customer. Defining a channel strategy is not a straight forward decision. All middlemen are in a sense in partnership with you to sell something to the end-user. Therefore, your product must be able to meet the turnover and margin needs of all the distribution intermediaries.

In setting your distribution strategy start at the point of final purchase. Who is the final consumer or user of your product? Where does that person go when buying your product category? If she buys this product from say a stationer, where does that retailer obtain his stock? When the various channels have been identified, it is simpler to determine which avenues make the most sense at the least cost.

In a broader context, 'place' can also relate to customer accessibility to you. In some cases, you need to question:
• Can customers negotiate and complete business transactions by telephone or via the Internet?
• Do customers have ready access to your sales personnel?
• Can customers in remote areas transact business with you via authorized agents or distributors?

The two broad options you can consider to access customers are 'direct' and 'indirect'. The routes you choose are determined to a large extent by the type of product or service you offer. Within the two broad categories numerous sub-categories exist. The next table lists the most common forms of direct and indirect distribution.

Using multiple channels of distribution

Depending on product or service category, you do not necessarily need to confine yourself to a single distribution channel to get your products to market. Indeed you should examine if there is room to 'cover all the bases'. Some organizations use a combination of direct and indirect distribution. For example Dell Computers successfully combines eCommerce with database marketing such as direct mail and mass email marketing. In some markets Dell has also branched into retail distribution via selected retail chains.

Some manufacturers use wholesalers in one or more geographical markets while using agents or distributors in others. Ultimately it comes down to who can offer the broadest market penetration at the least cost.

The internet through eCommerce has opened virtually unlimited opportunities to millions of businesses as an adjunct to existing distribution arrangements and has become an increasingly important option.

TABLE 9 - Distribution channels

DIRECT DISTRIBUTION

Channel	Examples	Advantages	Disadvantages
Direct to consumer via household contact	Avon, Tupperware	Product exclusivity	Limited consumer access
Service providers direct interface with customers	Tradesmen such as electricians, plumbers, etc.	Low overheads	Absence of passing trade
Direct to consumer via internet (eCommerce).	Airlines, hotels, books, wine, Dell computers, cosmetics, multi-product platforms such as eBay and Amazon	Avoids retail margins	Requires confidence in online purchasing
Direct to consumer via mail order catalogues and flyers	Department stores, and many other retail outlets.	Reaches customers in remote areas. Product exclusivity	Costly to produce and distribute. High wastage.
Direct to consumer via factory showroom	Footwear, furniture blinds, clothing confectionery	Eliminates 'the middle man'	Puts retailers offside
Manufacturer to business customers via sales force.	Commercial furniture, communications equipment	Simplifies custom design process	High overheads

INDIRECT DISTRIBUTION

Channel	Examples	Advantages	Disadvantages
Manufacturer to retail chains	Grocery chains, variety stores etc.	Central delivery and warehousing	At the mercy of buying power of major retailers
Manufacturer to wholesalers to retail	Stationery products, jewelry, auto accessories etc.	Amortizes distribution costs with other manufacturers	Priorities shared with other manufacturers
Manufacturer to agents or distributors to dealer networks	Specialty products.	Access to broad distribution with shared costs	Low priority for individual products
Manufacturer to dealer networks	Cars, computers, agricultural machinery.	Specialized technical expertise	Highly dependent on relatively few
Manufacturer to export agents	Furniture, floor coverings, white goods, textiles, machinery, pharmaceuticals.	Agents' knowledge of local markets and their established networks & contacts	Initial establishment costs can be disproportionate to incremental revenue

NOTE: This table is not intended to be a comprehensive list of all distribution channel options. There are many permutations of the channels shown while other new channels are constantly being introduced, particularly via the internet.

"If your products are not readily accessible in the marketplace, your potential customers will buy competitors' products that are more readily available"

Template 28 - Distribution channels checklist (example)				
Product	Target market	Existing distribution channels	Efficiency ranking 1 to 10	Proposed changes (if any)
Free standing executive desks (existing products)	Small to medium corporate customers	Direct to specialized office furniture retailers	6	We may phase out of this market if the launch of our proposed new work station module product line is successful
Work station modules (proposed product)	Small offices/Home offices	Direct to office furniture retailers, domestic furniture retailers, office supply chains and (later) Internet ecommerce marketing	Not yet tested	To be determined

4.3.3 Distribution Channel Partners Business Maximization

Business class	B2C Products ✔	B2B Products ✔	B2C Services X	B2B Services X
Plan level	Basic X	Intermediate X		Advanced ✔

To encourage your distribution channels to maximize the revenue they return, you need to service them and treat them as genuine 'partners'. Some of the ways in which you can achieve this include:

1. Treat them as an extension of your own sales force. Keep them informed about new developments on a day to day basis. Involve them in sales conferences and workshops. Give them access to your company's intranet and management systems. Accompany them on trade visits. Give them access to your market research data.

2. Provide them with selling tools to work with such as product samples, merchandising and sales materials.

3. Use both 'push' and 'pull' in their territories such as providing stock level and merchandising incentives to push your merchandise into their inventories while using media advertising or promotions to pull the stock out.

4. Set and agree sales and promotion budgets that are regularly reviewed.

5. Consider the offer of consignment stock when you are trying to get established.

Template 29 - Distribution channels partners maximization checklist (example)

Product	Distribution Channel	Proposed Development Strategies
Work station modules	Office supply chains	Build floor displays of assembled modules. Merchandise with quality point-of-sale materials
Work station modules	Domestic furniture retailers	As above
Work station modules	Office furniture retailers	Set up regular meetings for sales progress reviews. Invite key contacts to factory/showroom sales events.
Tables, seating, storage etc.	All existing channels	Maintain all current programs to sustain distribution of existing products as long as possible.

"Treat your distribution partners as an extension of your own sales force"

4.3.4 Supply Chain Management[1]

Business class	B2C Products ✔	B2B Products ✔	B2C Services ✗	B2B Services ✗
Plan level	Basic ✗	Intermediate ✗		Advanced ✔

Business location and distribution are closely linked with the relatively recent term 'supply chain management'.

A supply chain is a network of facilities and distribution options that performs the functions of procurement of materials, transformation of these materials into intermediate and finished products and the distribution of these finished products to customers.

Supply chain management focuses on the production and distribution of goods from raw materials to finished products in the hands of consumers in the best time and cost efficient manner possible.

Traditionally, marketing, distribution, planning, manufacturing, and the purchasing functions along with the supply chain operated independently.

These functions have their own objectives and are often conflicting.

---

1. NOTE: Supply chain management is a genuine marketing function because it can provide key benefits to retailers and consumers alike and can deliver important competitive advantages. It is a function often overlooked in other marketing plan development models.

Supply chain management is a means of making integration occur. In doing so, retailers, and through them consumers' needs can be more efficiently met with shorter more efficient lead times. Efficient supply chain management can often counter cheaper imported products and less efficient suppliers.

Shorter supply chains with improvements to shipping (or delivery) times can yield significant competitive advantages. Efficient manufacturers practice 'Just in time' (JIT) inventory which is a management system in which materials or products are produced or acquired only as demand requires. This approach to managing inventory has become increasingly important as suppliers and retailers collaborate to try to control inventory costs while still meeting customer demands.

Template 30 - Supply chain checklist (example)		
Supply chain stage	Existing efficiency rating (Scale 1 to 10)	Proposed changes to shorten the chain
Raw materials to factory	6	Keep tighter inventory control on raw materials stock levels at factory and place orders at predetermined trigger points
Factory to distribution channels	5	Maintain closer checks of finished product stock levels at distributors and agents and replenish stock levels before stock outs
Distribution channels to retailers	6	Keep closer controls on stock levels at retail level and ensure distributors and agents can supply stock at short notice
Factory to retailers	7	Closely monitor stock levels at retailers and ensure factory can supply direct orders within two working days. Implement 'just in time' inventory management system.

"Shorter supply chains can yield significant competitive advantages"

PROMOTION

Promotion is a generic term that involves communicating with the public in order to influence them to buy your products and/or services. It is an all-encompassing term that includes the many ways in which to create awareness of a product or service and to influence purchase.

The acronym AIDA represents the process of promotion:

Attention: Attract the prospect's attention

Interest: Gain the prospect's interest

Desire: Create the prospect's desire to purchase

Action: Lead the prospect to complete the purchase transaction

Some marketers have added an 'S' to denote the word 'Satisfaction' as in satisfying the customer through customer service so they become repeat purchasers.

Promotion can be expressed as 'above the line' or 'below the line'. Above the line refers to all expenditure on traditional media advertising such as in newspapers, magazines, TV, radio, outdoor or transportation advertising and social media advertising. 'Below the line' refers to all other promotional activities such as special offers, deals and allowances, point-of-sale advertising and merchandising, competitions and contests, publicity, personal selling, direct marketing, eCommerce, social media networking and many more.

Advances in social media platforms with their ability to accurately and cost effectively target specific target markets are seeing a shift from 'traditional' media to 'new' media – a trend that is of increasing significance to SME's.

4.4.1 Sales Force Management

Business class	B2C Products ✔	B2B Products ✔	B2C Services ✔	B2B Services ✔
Plan level	Basic X		Intermediate X	Advanced ✔

Micro businesses (fewer than five employees) and many SME's do not have the luxury of a sales department or even a dedicated salesman. The proprietors of these businesses often cover all the management function bases including sales. Typically in small businesses (those with less than twenty employees) one person combines the sales and marketing functions with other roles such as quoting, customer service and running the show room if there is one.

The sales management function involving the management of a sales force usually only applies in the case of SME's at the upper end of the scale (up to 100 employees) however the same principles of sales management apply regardless of the size of the enterprise.

Assuming the existence of a sales force whether staffed with telesales or sales representatives, or both, the key responsibilities of the sales manager are efficient deployment of the sales force and maximization of product distribution.

These considerations vary according to the size and organization of your internal sales force and how it is structured in relation to external agents and distributors according to the market in which you compete, the geographical area you cover and the channels of distribution applicable to your business.

An important role of the sales force is to get the retail trade and other channel intermediaries "on side". The benefits this can provide are wide and far reaching. Retailers often have the discretion to prominently display your product, allocate (disproportionate to sales) shelf space, price them competitively, and generally "push" your products in preference to competitive products competing for the same customers.

The management of call cycles is an important sales management function. How frequently should your sales people call on individual customers? Should the calls be face-to-face personal calls or telephone calls or a combination of both?

Template 31 - Sales management functions checklist (example)

Function	Efficiency rating (Scale of 1 to 10)	Proposed action
Sales reps coverage of potential market	6	We intend to increase sales representative coverage from 60% of available retail outlets to 80% with the addition of one more salesman to service retailers outside the main metropolitan area
Call cycle frequency	7	We will grade retailers by potential sales volume and structure sales calls accordingly. "A" grade stores will receive fortnightly calls. "B" grade stores will receive monthly calls and "C" grade stores will be allocated bimonthly calls.
Quality of sales reps calls	7	We will provide sales persons with up to date computer generated customer records so that they can present sales status to retail buyers with suggested improvement opportunities
Sales territory allocation efficiency	6	We will conduct regular reviews to ensure minimum sales territory overlaps.
Quality of service to retail trade	7	We will provide sales persons with quality materials to allow them to professionally present industry trends and new product updates.
Sales training	4	We have neglected this area of our operations and intend to appoint external sales trainers to conduct half yearly training workshops on different aspects of the sales function.

It is important to find the right balance between minimizing sales force costs while adequately servicing your customers' needs. Call cycles vary considerably from one product category to another and need to be reviewed on a regular basis.

Sales managers also need to review sales territories regularly to ensure that overlap and duplication is avoided. It is also part of a sales manager's function to plan sales call routes so that efficient use of sales representatives' time and travel is maximized as both are expensive overhead costs to the business.

"A key function of the sales force is to foster positive relationships with the retail trade"

4.4.2 Sales Development

Business class	B2C Products ✔	B2B Products ✔	B2C Services ✔	B2B Services ✔
Plan level	Basic ✔		Intermediate ✔	Advanced ✔

There are five primary sales development strategies.

1. Retaining existing customers

New business is incremental business only when existing customers are retained. Customer retention relies on maintaining customer satisfaction through the maintenance of uncompromising standards of customer service and product quality. It is six to seven times more expensive to attract a new customer than to retain an existing one.

2. Raise the average sales value

Would you like fries with that? Develop ways to increase the average dollar value of each sale e.g. raise an average $1000 sale to say $1200. For example if you are selling laptop computers offer discounted laptops carry cases or software.

3. Encourage repeat purchasing

Increase the incidence of repeat purchasing using 'customer loyalty' and other programs. This could be as simple as a providing a discount coupon on the next purchase with each sale. It is much less expensive to gain incremental business from existing customers than it is from new ones.

4. Reinstate lapsed customers

Lapsed customers often respond favorably to renewed contact especially if they have enjoyed a successful association with you in the past and have had unsatisfactory experiences with other suppliers since dealing with you.

5. Expand the customer base

New business is the lifeblood of any enterprise. Without it no business can survive. As existing customers lapse, it is essential they are replaced with new customers who are entering the market for the first time or switching from competitors.

The Sales Funnel Concept

Definition: *the buying process that companies lead customers through when purchasing products.* A sales funnel is divided into several steps, which differ according to the particular sales model in question. A typical sales funnel would have the following steps in a chain: Awareness (of your products or services) > Leads generated > Prospects > Customers. The role of marketing and sales management is to work to remove barriers to the sale by employing sales techniques and processes that are appropriate to the business model. Sales funnels can be managed by developing sales metrics that are appropriate to your business.

Customer Relationship Management

Definition: Customer relationship management (CRM) is a term that refers to practices, strategies and technologies that companies use to manage and analyze customer interactions, engagement and data throughout the customer lifecycle, with the goal of improving business relationships with customers, assisting in customer retention and driving sales growth. The system aims at improving the relationship with existing customers, finding new prospective customers, and winning back former customers. CRM often involves using specialized software program technology to organize, automate, and synchronize sales, marketing, customer service, operations, field service, project automation and technical support. All the data is stored in one central database allowing all business functions to access it easily from the cloud. The software is often used to automate various sales and marketing functions.

Sales Development Techniques - existing customers:

Up selling is persuading customers to buy a higher grade of a product or service they have already purchased. This technique is used by Microsoft and Symantec for example when new versions of computer programs and operating systems are introduced.

Cross selling is the term used when selling 'add-ons' to a product already purchased. For example a camera store salesman might sell a tripod, an external flash, a camera case and a wide angle lens to a customer who has already purchased a camera. Or a tire retailer who sells a wheel alignment or mag wheels to a customer when having tires fitted.

Volume discounts may be offered to persuade a customer to purchase more of the same product. For example a stationery salesman might offer a customer a volume discount to purchase a box of six reams of paper instead of just one.

Reward (or loyalty) programs are used to persuade customers to become repeat purchasers. For example each time a customer books a flight with an airline bonus points may be offered towards future flights.

Bundling is a technique that involves packaging a deal. For example a carpet cleaning company may offer a special deal for cleaning curtains and drapes as well as carpets.

Incremental selling can be used to persuade a customer to purchase an additional product or service to that which is already purchased. An example of this is a swimming pool company representative who sells a swimming pool fence or pool filters,to a customer who has had a pool installed.

There are many variations of these techniques limited only by your imagination.

Template 32 - Sales development techniques *existing* customers (example)	
Sales technique	Proposed actions
Up selling	Offer work station customers a 10% cash back offer to upgrade to new product releases
Cross selling	Offer work station purchasers a 10% cash back offer on office chairs
Volume discounts	Offer retailers a 15% discount for two or more work station modules with a 10% discount passed on to consumers.
Reward programs	Offer customers a free computer monitor arm on three consecutive purchases in a two year period.
Bundling	Offer work station customers a 5% discount on the purchase of a small side table bundled with a work station
Incremental selling	Offer work station customers a 20% cashback with an additional purchase of a work station screen
NOTE: Offers to existing customers will be communicated via our proposed database email marketing program	

Sales Development Techniques – new customers

In addition to advertising and internet marketing the three most common forms of new customers' sales development are:

Personal recommendation. Without exception the most effective form of sales development is personal recommendation and referrals from existing satisfied customers or third-party advocacy. People respond more readily to personal recommendations from people who have dealt with you than any other way. You may be able to encourage personal recommendation from satisfied customers to friends and family through discounts on future purchases, bonus offers and other reward concepts.

Cold canvassing. Development of cold canvassing techniques such as generating sales leads via door knocking, letterbox drops, direct mail, database email marketing, telesales and internet marketing.

Networking. Expansion of your contact list through networking among community groups has an important role in prospecting. Join clubs and community service organizations to expand your contacts and develop sales leads. Also seek public speaking opportunities in your area of expertise. Do not forget to take a generous supply of business cards!

> *"It is six to seven times more expensive to attract a new customer than to retain an existing one."*

Template 33 - Sales development techniques *new* customers (example)	
Sales technique	Proposed actions
Personal recommendation	We will offer existing customers a 10% discount on their next purchase when they 'refer a friend' that results in a work station purchase.
Cold canvassing	We will develop a cold canvassing program at retail level calling on potential stockists via personal selling, telesales and email marketing.
Networking	We will join the Small Business Association in our area with a view to delivering presentations and networking among other small business owner operators.
Advertising	We will advertise in selected newspapers and small business magazines.
Internet marketing	We will develop a first class interactive website and invest in search engine advertising.

"The most effective form of sales development is personal recommendation from existing satisfied customers.

4.4.3 Customer Service

Business class	B2C Products ✓	B2B Products ✓	B2C Services ✓	B2B Services ✓
Plan level	Basic ✓	Intermediate ✓		Advanced ✓

The sales and customer service functions are closely interrelated. Customer servicing refers to the backup, assistance and advice a business offers to its customers at every level of the distribution chain from wholesalers and agents through to retailers and the end consumer.

Servicing is an intangible benefit that a business can offer to secure competitive advantages.

What follows from poor customer service?
- Competitors can and do use it against you
- Other customers get to hear about it

- Relationships with your customers break down. They become disengaged with your company.
- You lose customers and your sales suffer.

In this digital age critical online reviews and blogs can reach a wide audience with devastating results. Conversely positive reviews can result in invaluable trusted endorsements.

What are the benefits of good customer service?
- Your competitors are disadvantaged.
- The good news spreads to other customers. Your customers become 'evangelists'.
- Customer relationships improve. They become engaged with your company and its brands.
- You retain your customer base through brand loyalty and generate incremental business.

What do you need to do to exceed customers' expectations?

Customer focus
1. Understand your customers business and needs.
2. Involve the customer in the service development process.
3. Be original in addressing your customers' needs.
4. Be committed to your customers' long-term success.
5. Provide on-going "value added" service to customers by anticipating their changing needs and delivering solutions.
6. Take initiatives. Do not wait to be asked before improving service levels.

Product knowledge
1. Develop an intimate knowledge of your products and services.
2. Know how you can use your products to meet and exceed your customers' needs.
3. Understand your competitors' products better than they do.
4. Know your competitive advantages and how to use them to your benefit

Customer Communications
1. Maintain regular contact with your customers. Don't wait for them to contact you or for a problem to arise
2. Prepare service calls thoroughly and anticipate their needs.
3. Do not say "no" without explaining the reason and volunteering an alternative solution
4. Always follow-up issues and report outcomes (feedback).
5. Confirm important decisions in writing
6. Listen intently to what your customers relate to you. There may be implicit hidden messages they are reluctant to enunciate.
7. Look for body language and other nuances which may indicate latent issues.
8. Use regular telephone or online customer service surveys to elicit valuable feed back.

Customer Relations

1. Gain your customers' complete confidence and trust
2. Honor your commitments – do what you say you are going to do
3. Make yourself indispensable to your customers
4. Create strategic alliances with your customers

Remember, existing customers are your biggest source of untapped profit. It is more cost effective to develop incremental business from existing customers than gaining new business from new customers. Ultimately it may be customer service not price that determines gaining and retaining customers for the long term.

"A customer is the most important visitor on our premises. He is not dependent on us. We are dependent on him. He is not an interruption to our work. He is the purpose of it. He is not an outsider to our business. He is part of it. We are not doing him a favor by serving him. He is doing us a favor by giving us an opportunity to do so" - Mahatma Gandhi [1]

Template 34 - Customer service action list (example)

Customer service functions	Efficiency rating (Scale 1 to 10)	Proposed actions
Customer focus	5	We intend to consult retail stockists in the development of the new range. We will assist them with merchandising and advertising. We will also conduct market research among potential end users
Product knowledge	6	We will communicate our products advantages over the competition to retail stockists and end users. We will supply buyers with regular updates on market segment trends.
Customer communications	7	We will maintain close liaison with retail stockists to ensure they are carrying adequate but not excessive stocks. We will make sure we maintain a customer contact schedule that suits their individual needs. We will maintain a dedicated help section in our website and have a free call consumer advice facility.
Customer relations	7	We will honor our commitments to our trade customers to the letter and assist them wherever possible to improve their turnover in the product category. We will also provide end users with 12 month warranties on workmanship and parts.

"Always treat the customer as an appreciating asset."
- Tom Peters, Business Author

---

[1]. Author's note: I have often wondered why Mahatma Gandhi of all people would have had an involvement in customer relations. However as strange as it seems he is widely credited with this quote so I must assume it is correctly attributed to him.

4.5 Advertising

As outrageous as it sounds, most of the money spent on advertising is wasted. This can be due to any number of reasons from poor planning or execution to insufficient allocation of funds, placement in inappropriate media or inadequate branding registration. How often do you see an advertisement or commercial which has no clear product proposition or positioning, that is devoid of a memorable 'big idea' and is so bland that it gets completely lost in the avalanche of advertising we are all exposed to every single day?

Conversely, when planning and execution are soundly based, advertising results can be spectacular.

It must be said that advertising does not produce miracles. You soon get caught out if the advertising claims are not delivered by the product or service. But when the right product is sold at the right price in the right place and at the right time and communicated in the right way, advertising can and does provide a sometimes quite remarkable impetus to sales.

Advertising is the most visible and often the most costly part of your marketing program. It is a multifaceted branch of marketing that combines strategic and creative development, media selection and placement, media production and advertising research among others.

It is a mass medium that usually has a significant wastage factor in reaching people exposed to the message but who are 'not in the market' for the advertised product or service being advertised.

Micro and small businesses should use mass media advertising with caution as it exhausts modest budgets often with nothing to show for it. It is less suitable for business to business marketing where direct marketing strategies are more cost effective. Media advertising is more appropriate for business to consumer enterprises (B2C) marketing products that are consumed day to day and where the target market is hard to reach by more direct means.

Depending on the size of your advertising budget and the place of advertising in your overall marketing mix, the options are to appoint an advertising agency to assist you or to coordinate the advertising component of the plan internally. (Refer introductory notes).

As a general rule, advertising agencies cater for businesses with big budgets. If your budget is less than six figures in $US you will probably not get the level of service you need.

All too often, an advertising budget is regarded as discretionary expenditure. When market conditions are tight, the advertising budget is often the first cost to be slashed. Yet advertising and promotion is a 'cost of doing business' just as much as production and administration.

Advertising should be regarded as a fixed cost - not as a discretionary item to cut at the first sign of slowing sales. This is the very time you need to consider increasing your advertising profile and visibility.

The Six Step Process
Advertising can be broken down to a six step process:
1) Setting the advertising objectives
2) Allocating responsibility
3) Setting the advertising budget
4) The creative brief and execution evaluation
5) Media selection and placement
6) Advertising research

4.5.1 Setting the Advertising Objectives

Business class	B2C Products ✔	B2B Products ✔	B2C Services ✔	B2B Services ✔
Plan level	Basic ✔		Intermediate ✔	Advanced ✔

Before you can think about how to do it you need to understand what you want advertising to realistically achieve.

Advertising can produce spectacular results but only if all of the other components of product, place, price and promotion are aligned. Your product or service has to meet consumers' needs or wants, at the right price, in the right place and communicate the message in the right way to the right people. When these basics are in place define exactly what you want advertising to achieve.

The more specific you are about defining the advertising objectives as a subset of the marketing objectives the more likely you are to achieve them. It is not sufficient to say your advertising objective is to "increase sales". All advertising is intended to increase sales but there are usually more specific things you need to achieve in order for sales to be increased.

Here are some specifics that advertising can realistically achieve:
Create brand and product awareness
Announce a new store location
Build store traffic
Launch a new product
Stimulate product trial
Persuade consumers that your product is better than the competition
Generate sales enquiries
Demonstrate a product
Communicate a new improved feature
Build a brand image
Communicate product positioning and product propositions
Drive prospective customers to your website.

Advertising may be required to meet two or more objectives. Generally it is preferable to define just one primary objective with any others set as secondary objectives, in order of importance, so that the relative priority is clear to everyone involved. As with all objectives it is desirable to set a time frame and indicate how you will measure achievement to assess your level of success.

Template 35 - Setting the advertising objectives (example)	
Advertising Objective	How measured
PRIMARY Generate sales enquiries and convert enquiries to sales at the six principal retail stockists.	Sales recorded by each of the six principal stockists within two months of each advertising cycle.
SECONDARY 1 Gain prominent display space support from retail stockists by directing store traffic to them from our advertising and cooperative trade advertising.	We will maintain a register of retail display floor space allocated by each of the retailers listed in print advertisements, before, during and after advertising scheduling.
SECONDARY 2 Create interest and enquiries from retailers not currently stocking our products	We will create and maintain a database system that will record all stages of sales development from initial contact to customer conversion.

"Half the money I spend on advertising is wasted. The problem is I never know which half" – Lord Leverhulme. Founder of Lever Bros

4.5.2 Advertising Responsibilities Allocation

Business class	B2C Products ✔	B2B Products ✔	B2C Services ✔	B2B Services ✔
Plan level	Basic X		Intermediate ✔	Advanced ✔

In micro to small businesses the proprietor or manager is usually responsible for coordinating the firm's advertising program along with just about everything else. In a medium enterprise advertising is often the responsibility of the sales manager.

Specialist marketing managers are usually part of the corporate structure at the upper end of medium enterprises and in large corporations.

Depending on the size of the budget you will need to determine if you will create the advertising material 'in-house', use the creative services of the media with which the advertising is placed or (if the budget warrants) appoint an advertising agency. (Refer 'Introductory notes' for more information).

In any case the marketing plan should be specific about precisely who is responsible for each part of the process so that there is no misunderstanding.

Template 36 - Advertising responsibilities allocation (examples)		
Advertising function	Scheduled completion date	Person responsible
Advertising budget allocation	Mid 2017	Mark (with Dennis' approval)
Setting the advertising brief	September 2017	Mark
Media selection	September 2017	Mark
Allocation of creative resources and development of creative material	October 2017	Mark
Advertising material approval	January 2018	Mark
Media placement	April 2018	Mark

4.5.3 Setting the Advertising Budget

Business class	B2C Products ✔	B2B Products ✔	B2C Services ✔	B2B Services ✔
Plan level	Basic ✔		Intermediate ✔	Advanced ✔

Setting the advertising budget is never straight forward as there is no standard formula. You will need to consider a number of factors before you can arrive at an acceptable spend level.

Big companies with big budgets often determine advertising spend levels with cost estimates of what would be required to achieve set impact objectives such as reach and frequency[1] and target audience ratings points (TARPS)[2] against the target market. This approach is not practical for SME's where the budgets would be too small to be measurable or meaningful.

Practical considerations are:

• Allocate an affordable fixed percent of budgeted revenue. This is often around five to six percent but can be much more in the case of low cost/high margin products such as cosmetics, skin care and hair care products.

• In the case of established enterprises past spend levels compared with the response received can give you a rough guide as to what you need to spend to achieve your objectives.

• Estimate what it would cost on a budget line-by-line basis to reach your sales and profit goals.

• Estimate how much your competitors spend on marketing and then allocate a proportionate amount based on relative market share.

---
1. Reach refers to the number of persons in the target market (expressed as a percentage) who are exposed to the advertising message in a given schedule while the frequency is the average number of times the target market sees or hears the message
2. TARPS is an acronym for Target Audience Rating Points and is calculated by multiplying reach by frequency.

- Determining the level of 'investment' that is acceptable in the overall corporate budget.

When setting the final budget figure consider all of the above overlaid with common commercial sense to achieve the most practical balance.

Do not fritter money or effort on trying to do too much. It is more effective to concentrate the budget on a few carefully selected high priority items (and do them well) than to attempt to spread the spend level over too many items (and not do anything adequately) in an attempt to 'cover all the bases'.

The practicality of the advertising budget along with all other marketing budget items will be assessed in the financial statement in terms of its practicality and 'fit' with corporate goals and objectives.

Template 37 – Setting the advertising budget (example)

Considerations	Comments
Fixed % of budgeted revenue	Based on gross revenue of $1.3M, (existing and new products) we have resolved that we are prepared to spend up to 37% of gross revenue on marketing in year 1 to establish the new product range. Within this we will invest around 7% of gross revenue on advertising. This equates to an advertising budget of $91,000
Acceptable investment level	We consider that an initial advertising budget of $91,000 is an acceptable investment in advertising in Year 1. We have allocated a reserve of $39,000 in the overall marketing budget, which will be added to the advertising budget if budgeted revenue remains on track or if it is exceeded. This would create a maximum advertising budget of 10% of gross sales.
Past spend levels	We have not advertised to any extent in the past.
Cost estimate on a line by line basis of media and production costs	We have estimated that the budget allocated is adequate to fund the scale of advertising we require to achieve the set objectives.
Competitors' spend levels	We do not yet have any direct competitors with whom to compare spend levels.
Advertising budget allocation ($'s)	Up to a maximum of $100,000 in year 1 (including contingency).

4.5.4 Preparing the Creative Brief and Execution Evaluation

Business class	B2C Products ✔	B2B Products ✔	B2C Services ✔	B2B Services ✔
Plan level	Basic ✔	Intermediate ✔		Advanced ✔

Whether you are creating the advertising 'in house' or assigning the task to external resources, the starting point in the creative process is to ensure that the brief is strategically sound. This requires clarity in defining the task and the resources available. It is important that you get this clear in your own mind at the outset and to commit it succinctly to a single sheet of paper.

Based on your first-hand knowledge of the business it is the advertiser's role to define the objectives, the target market, the product positioning and proposition, the desired brand image and the net impression to be left with the target market.

The discipline required in thinking these elements through will make the evaluation of the creative execution clearer and so much easier to assess.

The brief can certainly and should be agreed or debated by the creative resource with the advertiser at the outset, but once mutually agreed the task of the creative resource is to deliver an inspired interpretation that meets the brief and delivers 'cut through' with a 'big idea' that stands out in the crowd.

The responsibility for spending the budget cost efficiently rests with you — the advertiser — after all it is your money — not the agency's or the media with whom you are placing the advertising. You therefore need to be clear about whether the creative execution is on strategy and meets the brief or not.

If you have any doubts about the execution meeting the brief, stand your ground and demand to see other creative options. David Ogilvy, the noted advertising expert, famously said, "You will never win fame and fortune unless you invent big ideas. It takes a big idea to attract the attention of consumers and get them to buy your product. Unless your advertising contains a big idea, it will pass like a ship in the night."

Template 38 - The creative brief (example)

Product or service:	SoHo workstation modules
Overall marketing objective:	Create and dominate a new product segment in our home market.
Primary advertising objective:	Create consumer awareness, generate sales enquiries and convert enquiries to sales at the six designated principal retail stockists
Secondary advertising objective:	Gain prominent display space and sales support from stockists by directing sales traffic to them from our advertising
Target market:	Small office/home office decision makers who are early adopters of new high-end technology.
Product proposition:	"SoHo work stations deliver higher productivity in less floor space".
Product positioning:	Cutting edge work stations for the small office/home office
Desired brand image:	Technologically advanced, premium quality, flexible in use
Desired net impression:	The ultimate in small office/home office furniture for advanced users of computer technology
Advertising budget:	The total ad budget is up to a maximum of $100,000 for Year 1

4.5.5 Media Selection

Business class	B2C Products ✔	B2B Products ✔	B2C Services ✔	B2B Services ✔
Plan level	Basic ✔	Intermediate ✔	Advanced ✔	

Effective advertising requires not only the right message but also the right medium (or mix of media) to get that message across to a tightly defined target audience. Media selection is one of the most critical aspects of successful advertising and cannot be overstated.

The same advertising campaign placed in the right medium or media for the target market will be infinitely more effective than the same budget spent on advertising in the wrong media.

Media selection is the process of determining the most cost effective medium or set of media to reach and engage your tightly defined target market. You need to be able to make sure that the target market knows about the product, develops an interest in its features and knows where to buy it.

Each medium has its own set of advantages and disadvantages. For example if it is important to show the product use visual media. If the strategy is to offer consumers special discount coupons use print media. If you need to promote a retail site use outdoor advertising. If you need to reach customers in a localized area consider localized newspapers. If you need an audio/visual medium to reach a mass market use TV advertising. If you need to reach teenagers and young adults use social media advertising such as in Facebook, Twitter and YouTube.

Another aspect to consider is placement within a medium and even within the same TV or radio station programming or newspaper or magazine position. For example placement in different TV programs and time zones and within different sections of a newspaper deliver entirely different target audiences.

The key is to reach the maximum number of people in the primary target market with minimum wastage. Another factor to consider is the cost of reaching the target market. Most media will be able to give you an estimate of the number of people in a particular target audience you will be able to reach with a given advertising budget.

Also remember that advertising generally needs enough 'opportunities to see' before it begins to register with the target market. It is generally recognized that at least five opportunities to see are needed before any impact is registered and much more if the objective is to build brand imagery and to bring about brand switching. To achieve a given number of opportunities to see you will need considerably more radio or TV transmissions or newspaper or magazine advertisement insertions.

Another point to remember is that it is a mistake to change an advertisement too often as most people are only just becoming aware of an advertising message when the advertiser is becoming bored with it.

Also bear in mind the rapidly rising trend of social media advertising due to its accurate targeting ability at the expense of traditional media such as TV, radio and newspapers. Depending on your target market, social media advertising may be the better cost effective option. The challenge is to find the right balance.

To re-emphasize, one of the golden rules to remember in advertising is *do not fritter money or effort*. It is better to concentrate your budget in one or two media that reach your target market cost effectively than to spread your funds too thinly across many media.

If your budget warrants, it can be beneficial to engage the services of media consultants who can expertly advise on media selection, negotiate the best rates and place the advertising on your behalf.

The advertising media selection reference guide (Table 10) will help you to select the most appropriate media for the task at hand.

Template 39 - Media selection checklist (example)

Product: SoHo modular work stations		
☑ Cost effective reach of target market	☑ Retention of ads for future reference	☑ Ability to offer discount or other offer coupons
☑ Show the product	☑ List product stockists	☑ High impact
☒ Color	☒ Sound (audio)	☒ Movement (video)
☑ Short lead times	☑ Low production costs	☑ List product benefits
☑ List product specifications	☑ Response rate measurement	☑ Repetition
Preferred media option/s ☒TV ☒ Radio ☑ Newspapers ☑ Magazines ☒ Outdoor ☒ Cinema ☑ Cooperative trade advertising ☑ Social media advertising ☒ Third party websites ☒ Search engine advertising ☑ *Yellow pages and* other directories ☒ Other (Specify)		
Geographical markets we need to reach: San Diego and surrounding districts		
Budget allocated: Up to a maximum of $100,000 in Year 1		
Conclusions: Print media meets our criteria more efficiently than electronic media. We envisage a mix of ads in local newspapers supplemented with participation in cooperative retailers advertising and catalogs. We will experiment with social media advertising as this medium is appropriate to reach our tech savvy millennials target market.		

POWERFUL PROVEN WORDS IN ADVERTISING

'New' 'Now' 'Free' 'Fun' 'Save' 'Value' 'Guarantee' 'Healthy' 'Easy' 'Achieve' 'Dependable' 'Instant' 'How to' 'Love' 'Proven' 'Quality' 'Results' 'Safe' 'Secure' 'Simple' 'Solution' 'Step by step' 'Strong' 'Top' 'Uncover' 'Unique' 'Unlimited' 'Unlock' 'Discover' 'Winning' 'Yes' 'Better' 'Superior'

TABLE 10 – Media selection reference guide

Media	Advantages	Disadvantages
Television	<ul><li>The most powerful advertising mass medium.</li><li>Combines vision/sound/movement</li><li>Appealing to senses</li><li>Commands high attention levels</li><li>Wide mass market audience reach</li><li>Selective on a national/state/regional level</li></ul>	<ul><li>High cost both in terms of air time and production</li><li>Large clutter and waste factor</li><li>Needs repetition</li><li>Limits on information that can be provided</li><li>Long ad breaks lead to viewer 'turn off'</li></ul>
Newspapers	<ul><li>Flexible in ad size and shape</li><li>Can target large or small geographic areas</li><li>Immediate results</li><li>Very short lead times</li><li>In-house production facilities usually available</li><li>Full color facilities widely available</li><li>Very suitable for retail advertising</li><li>Ads easily clipped for future reference</li><li>Often carry preprinted inserts as an economical distribution method.</li></ul>	<ul><li>Transient – 24 hour life maximum for dailies</li><li>Considerable clutter</li><li>High waste factor on readers not in the target market</li><li>Production costs can be high</li></ul>
Radio	<ul><li>High target audience selectivity</li><li>The "medium of the mind" (allows listeners to use imagination)</li><li>Low cost (relative to TV)</li><li>Rates usually negotiable</li><li>Relatively low production costs</li></ul>	<ul><li>As an audio medium not suitable for food appetite appeal, pack identification, etc.</li><li>Fleeting exposure – needs repetition.</li><li>No retention facility</li><li>Commercials often 'lost' in multi commercial ad breaks</li></ul>
Magazines	<ul><li>High target audience selection options</li><li>High quality color reproduction</li><li>Long life</li><li>Good 'pass along" readership</li><li>Good reader involvement</li><li>Even small ads not overlooked</li></ul>	<ul><li>Long lead times</li><li>Intense competition from competing ads.</li><li>Expensive space costs</li></ul>
Outdoor Advertising (e.g. hoardings, transport, etc.)	<ul><li>Very flexible by location</li><li>Relatively low cost per reader</li><li>Relatively long life</li><li>High visibility according to size and position</li></ul>	<ul><li>Limitations on length of message</li><li>High maintenance</li><li>High production costs</li><li>Limited 'readership' data available</li><li>Response rates difficult to measure</li></ul>
Cinema	<ul><li>Effective in reaching younger age groups less likely to be exposed to other media</li><li>Effective in reaching localized audiences</li></ul>	<ul><li>Production costs (other than slideshows) can be prohibitive unless adapted from TV material</li></ul>
Social media advertising (e.g. Facebook, YouTube, Twitter etc.)	<ul><li>Highly accurate targeting. Can be filtered by location, demographics, interests, behaviors, connections and custom audiences.</li><li>Can reach young tech savvy audiences not exposed to traditional media.</li><li>Can use multi-media such as videos and blogs</li><li>Ads can go viral</li></ul>	<ul><li>High levels of competition</li><li>Maintenance requires considerable time and resources</li><li>Can result in negative comments</li><li>Can be difficult to catch attention due to clutter</li></ul>
Banner or Display advertising (in third party websites)	<ul><li>Accurate targeting potential</li><li>Multimedia technology can provide high visibility and innovation</li><li>Ability to link to own website</li></ul>	<ul><li>Can be intrusive and considered as 'clutter'</li><li>Can be expensive relative to audience reach</li></ul>
Search Engine Advertising (e.g. AdWords).	<ul><li>Extremely flexible</li><li>Cost effective (pay per click)</li><li>Accurate targeting</li><li>Immediacy</li></ul>	<ul><li>Requires expert management for optimization</li><li>Costs vary by category and according to competition</li></ul>
Yellow Pages and other directories	<ul><li>Response rates relatively easy to measure</li><li>Year long life</li><li>Readers are in a buying mode</li><li>On line as well as hard copy</li></ul>	<ul><li>High clutter and competition</li><li>High rate costs</li><li>Not suitable for all business classes</li></ul>

"If you are lucky enough to write a good advertisement, repeat it until it stops selling. Scores of good ads are discarded before they lose their potency".   David Ogilvy

4.5.6 Advertising Research

Business class	B2C Products ✔	B2B Products ✔	B2C Services ✔	B2B Services ✔
Plan level	Basic ✔	Intermediate ✔		Advanced ✔

Many sophisticated research techniques have been developed for advertising *pre* and *post* testing. As the terms imply, *pretesting* is testing the advertising message before the advertising is run while *post* testing is measuring the response and comprehension after the advertising is run. However as these are required to be conducted by highly trained specialists the costs are generally prohibitive for the average SME. Alternatively, the following low or no cost methods are suggested:

Measure store traffic

Effectiveness of retail 'sale' advertising is self-evident by the immediate volume of additional store traffic generated by the advertising. Unlike brand image advertising, retail advertising must by definition produce an immediate result.

Discount coupons

Placed in newspaper ads, direct mail pieces, fliers or letter box drops, coupons offer a discount incentive upon presentation. Radio advertising can use a variation of this in which the customer is requested to mention hearing the offer on a specific radio station to redeem the offer.

Dedicated telephone numbers

Dedicated telephone numbers can be an efficient method to measure the number of consumer enquiries generated from newspaper, magazine or directory advertisements.

Simple customer surveys

If you are designing a questionnaire for general customer research into your company or products, always include questions relating to the media respondents read, view and listen to and ask questions relating to how they came to hear about you.

Talk to customers

As simple as it may sound, just asking customers how they came to hear about you or a particular offer you have made, can be very enlightening. Most people are more than happy to give you this kind of feedback. Anecdotal evidence while not definitive can be extremely valuable.

Website 'hits'

Sudden improvements in website hit numbers should be apparent during and immediately after advertising scheduling. You can record and analyze these to measure advertising impact and adjust your scheduling accordingly.

Advertising research does not have to be sophisticated and expensive to be illuminating

Template 40 - Advertising research checklist (example)	
Method	Comments
Measure store traffic before and after advertising	We will actively seek and monitor retailers feedback
Discount and cashback coupons	We will experiment with cashback offers in selected print media to gauge response rates
Dedicated telephone hotline number	We will have a dedicated hotline phone number to measure the Yellow Pages advertising response rate
Customer surveys	We will consider implementing a customer survey in the second year which will include questions relating to how customers became aware of our products
Seek customers feedback	We will conduct a telephone survey to measure advertising awareness upon receipt of customers' warranty cards.
Website 'hits'	We will use Google Analytics to measure website 'hit's before during and after advertising scheduling.

4.6 Sales Promotion

Business class	B2C Products ✔	B2B Products ✔	B2C Services ✔	B2B Services ✔
Plan level	Basic ✔		Intermediate ✔	Advanced ✔

Sales promotion (below the line) is the term used to describe all the activities you devise to increase sales apart from media advertising (above the line). The main objective of sales promotion is to provide consumers with an additional reason to purchase and to stimulate product trial.

Various forms of sales promotions can be targeted against customers, the sales force and the retail trade.

Sales promotions should be regarded as more tactical in nature than strategic. They are put in place to achieve short-term goals (up to three months in duration) as compared with media advertising, which has more of a long-term cumulative effect. An exception to this is retail advertising of the kind used to promote a sale or a short-term special offer.

The scope of sales promotion is almost open ended. It embraces such diverse activities as:
- Special discounts offered for the limited time of the promotion
- Sweepstakes - a type of lottery in which participants supply proof of purchase to go into a prize draw.
- Introductory offers such as a new restaurant may offer free entrées with every main course purchased.
- Loss leaders such as specific products sold at a slight loss in order to attract store traffic.
- Coupons such as those which offer free fries with every Big Mac.

- Banded packs such as a toothbrush banded with a tube of tooth paste for the regular price of one or the other.
- Competitions and contests such as coloring competitions or 'tell us in five words or less why you like Product X'.
- Trade and sales force incentive schemes in which prizes are offered for meeting or exceeding sales budgets.
- Premium offers such as a free tie with every suit purchased.
- Product catalogues such as those produced by department and chain stores.
- Trade shows and exhibitions such as boat, car and furniture exhibitions.
- In store sampling and displays such as free tastings of new or improved products.
- Distributing branded promotional merchandise such as caps, T-shirts, umbrellas etc.
- Related item promotions such as a discounted Coke tumbler with every McDonald's meal purchased.

Promotions can vary from the simplistic "blackboard offer" or letter box drop to a full scale nationally advertised consumer promotion.

Large-scale promotions are often devised and managed by specialized promotion agencies that operate in much the same way that advertising agencies coordinate media advertising.

Because promotions have a more immediate effect than media advertising it is easier to analyze and measure responses, experiment with different formats and offers and to arrive at successful formulas.

Template 41 - Sales promotion planning schedule (example)

Product: SoHo work modular stations

Objective	Promotion type	Timing & duration	Budget $'s	Coordin-ator
Create retail trade awareness & interest	Hold a product launch function for retailers to sell the new range	End 2016	10,000	Mark
Gain distribution and floor displays in retail stockists	Provide cash incentives and allowances for product listings and floor displays on a selective basis.	Two week promotions each quarter in the first year	30,000	Mark
Maintain trade and consumer interest and sales impetus	Periodic price reductions tied in with retailers advertising and promotions.	Two week promotions tied in with retail promotions and floor displays	20,000	Mark
Demonstrate the functionality and ease of assembly of the new product line to the trade and end users.	Produce a promotional DVD for use at trade shows and displays at selected retail stockists.	On a selective rotating basis	10,000	Mark
Establish and maintain awareness of the brand and product range	Produce a supply of promotional merchandise such as branded caps, T-Shirts, diaries and calendars.	In the initial four week product launch period	5,000	Mark

TABLE 11 - Consumer Promotion Concepts

Promotion Concepts	Advantages	Disadvantages
Consumer competitions, sweepstakes and contests	<ul><li>Can provide short term impetus to sales</li><li>High immediacy</li><li>Can be used strategically to tie in with high or low sales periods</li><li>Can gain "first time" buyers</li></ul>	<ul><li>Sales impetus stops immediately at end of promotion</li><li>Requires high levels of advertising and merchandising support</li><li>Special packaging costs expensive</li></ul>
In Store samplings and demonstrations	<ul><li>Interactive communication with potential buyers in a buying environment</li><li>High sales conversion rate</li><li>Favorably regarded by retail trade</li><li>Can be tied in with temporary price reductions for additional incentive</li></ul>	<ul><li>Labor intensive</li><li>Requires specialized trained personnel</li><li>Requires close supervision and coordination</li></ul>
Temporary price reductions	<ul><li>Provides trial purchase opportunities leading to repeat purchasing</li></ul>	<ul><li>High cost</li><li>Leads to lack of brand loyalty with consumers always buying the current brand "on special"</li></ul>
Special offers (e.g. "buy one get one free")	<ul><li>Can attract new users to segment/product/brand</li></ul>	<ul><li>High cost.</li><li>Difficult to manage</li><li>Requires special inventory</li><li>Specially marked costs expensive/difficult to administer</li></ul>
Banded (or bonus packs) (e.g. toothbrush banded with a tube of toothpaste)	<ul><li>Promotes impulse purchases</li><li>Attracts first time purchases</li><li>Creates additional merchandising and display opportunities,</li></ul>	<ul><li>Presents inventory control and supply chain issues</li><li>Does not always result in brand loyalty. Consumers revert back to original brands after expiration of offer</li></ul>
Accumulative points schemes (e.g. Fly buys)	<ul><li>Promotes consumer loyalty</li><li>Reduces price comparison shopping</li></ul>	<ul><li>Difficult and expensive to administer</li><li>Consumers can be skeptical of value</li></ul>
Premium offers (e.g. free tie with every suit purchased)	<ul><li>Provides a 'value added' advantage</li><li>Provides merchandising and display opportunities</li></ul>	<ul><li>Incremental administration and inventory costs.</li></ul>

NOTE: This table is representative of the most common promotion types but is far from comprehensive. New concepts and variations are constantly being introduced.

"Sales promotions are more tactical in nature than strategic"

4.7 Trade Shows and Exhibitions

Business class	B2C Products ✔	B2B Products ✔	B2C Services ✔	B2B Services ✔
Plan level	Basic X		Intermediate ✔	Advanced ✔

Trade shows and exhibitions are another legitimate form of sales promotion – particularly for consumer durable products such as furniture, appliances, information technology, automobiles, trailers, boats, antiques, swimming pools and spas etc.

Because these are mainly "big ticket" consumer durable items, they are more of a considered purchase than fast moving consumer goods (FMCG) such as supermarket products.

Visitors like the convenience of being able to look at and compare all the available options under one roof instead of having to go from one store to another.

Exhibitions are also a valuable way to reach the retail trade as they are well attended by retail buyers who can see your products in favorable circumstances and they can more easily allocate the time needed to gather all the information they require. Some shows allocate special days for the trade which preclude the general public.

Trade shows and exhibitions are suitable for selective B2C and B2B businesses.

Template 42- Trade shows & exhibitions schedule (example)			
Product	SoHo work station modules		
Trade show name	FURNITEX office furniture exhibition		
Target market	Retail trade buyers and Small office/home office workers		
Objective	Present the new range to the retail trade and potential end users		
Proposed activities	We will reserve a small stand to display assembled SoHo work station modules, demonstrate the product's features and screen the proposed promotional DVD. We will also use the event to write orders and provide trade hospitality.		
Timing & duration		Budget $'s	Coordinator
March 10 -17, 2019		15,000	Mark

Trade shows can be valuable in reaching the retail trade while exhibitions reach the broader public

TABLE 12 - Trade shows & exhibitions advantages/disadvantages
Advantages
Reach a predisposed audience with special interest in the product category
Ideal for products requiring demonstrations and technical detailing
Good for developing sales leads
Can be combined with customer entertainment
Can be used as a sales channel
Good source of contacts for database marketing
Good for competitive comparisons
Ideal for audio visual shows and demonstrations
Contact can be established with potential suppliers and importers
Disadvantages
Labor intensive
Travel, accommodation, and entertainment cost add-ons
Rent, fit out, labor and sales literature costs
Not suitable for all product categories

4.8 On-line Marketing and eCommerce

No other influence has had a more profound effect on marketing in decades than the explosive force of the internet. On-line or eCommerce interaction with customers has transformed the face of marketing. Now a quality website is not merely an adjunct to marketing activities — it is arguably your single most important marketing tool. A well-designed site with the right content and promotion brings your products within reach of not just the city or country you operate in — but opens a 24/7 gateway to the world.

A quality website allows you to provide access to your business to customers anywhere. It gives them immediate reference to your products and services and what your company stands for. It can tell people about your business philosophies, it can profile your key executives and provide an immediate source of two way communications through email.

Increasingly, businesses are using the web not just as an on-line 'corporate brochure' or a products or services 'showroom' but also as a means of facilitating actual on-line transactions. This is known as eCommerce. Now anyone can buy anything from anyone, anywhere at any time — all at a click of a mouse (and a credit card).

This has changed the entire mind-set in which we previously conducted business and smart operators are increasingly tapping into markets that were hitherto unthinkable.

4.8.1 Website Functionality

Business class	B2C Products ✓	B2B Products ✓	B2C Services ✓	B2B Services ✓
Plan level	Basic ✓		Intermediate ✓	Advanced ✓

The first thing to determine is what you want your website to do. Is it to inform prospects about your products or services to generate sales enquiries? Is it to create databases for sales leads? Is it to conduct eCommerce sales transactions through the Internet?

When you have the answers to these questions, you can start designing (or re-designing) your website. This means briefing an experienced web designer with a comprehensive brief that details the desired content and functionality of the site.

Remember your site is a reflection of your business. That is why it pays to get a professional designer to put it together. An unimpressive amateur site can actually create a poor image for your business and turn people away.

When you have a quality site that accurately represents your company and has all the functions required you need to start actively promoting the site.

Uploading your site to the web is not the end of the project but merely the beginning. There are literally millions of sites on the Internet. A website is useless no matter how original it is if it is lost in cyberspace and not receiving any 'hits'.

As with all other promotional tools, your site needs to be updated almost daily and brought to your prospects attention. This is where content marketing comes in. This involves creating and distributing valuable, relevant and consistent content to attract and acquire a clearly defined audience – with the objective of driving profitable customer action. It can include text (blogs, eBooks, press releases and tweets), video, audio and online events.

It is also a 'no brainer' to use Google Analytics which is a free platform that allows you to measure and analyze your website traffic. It tells you the number of 'hits' your site is receiving on a daily basis and breaks the data down to geographical locations, demographics, page views, time on the site, referrals sources, AdWords results, SEO information, and much more.

This information will guide you to fine tune the site to make it an increasingly effective marketing tool (which is a never ending process).

"A good quality, functional website is your single most important marketing tool"

MARKETING STRATEGIES

Template 43 - Website functionality requirements (example)

Product: SoHo modular work stations	
What functions do we require from our website?	☑ Showcase our products ☑ Generate sales enquiries via contact links ☑ Create databases for sales leads ☑ Conduct ecommerce transactions via the Internet ☑ Content management system ☑ Database email marketing facility ☐ Other
Contents checklist	☑ Product range catalogue ☑ Competitive advantages list ☑ Company history, mission statement and executives profiles ☑ email contact facility ☑ Shopping cart facility ☑ Credit card transaction facilities
Content marketing	Continually create and post items of interest such as: ☑ Blogs, ☑ eBooks, ☑ Press releases and other text based items of interest to our target market as well as ☑ Videos and podcasts
Action checklist	☑ Determine and assemble content ☑ Register web address ☑ Engage website designer ☑ Appoint internet service provider ☑ Appoint web server ☑ Arrange merchant (credit card transaction) facilities ☑ Exchange links with complementary sites
Maintenance checklist	☑ Continually improve and update web graphics and content ☑ Continually improve products/ services featured on the site ☑ Continue to seek new links with complementary sites ☑ Continue to place strategic advertising on search engines/analyze results/refine markets/budgets and key words ☑ Measure website traffic data with Google Analytics and make adjustments based on the data reported.

"Unique content is an important part of SEO"

4.8.2 Website Promotion Strategies

Business class	B2C Products ✔	B2B Products ✔	B2C Services ✔	B2B Services ✔
Plan level	Basic ✔		Intermediate ✔	Advanced ✔

It is pointless to go to great trouble and expense to develop a web site if no one visits it. That would be like running a bricks-and-mortar store without any customer traffic. You need to work hard and use a variety of strategies to attract visitors to your site. Here are some of the practical methods you can employ to encourage potential customers to log in to your web address.

1. Include your web address in all your stationery, such as business cards and letterheads. Also make sure it is prominently featured in your sales materials, advertising and signage.

2. Include your web address in your email signatures.

3. Offer to exchange links with websites with related interests.

4. Develop a presence in social media platforms such as Facebook and Twitter that are popular with your target market. Ensure that these entries have adequate links to your web address.

5. Visit all the major search engine sites and submit the URL of your web address to each one. Most search engines have a "submit URL facility" or a similar option.

6. The more quality content in your site the more it will be picked up and listed in search engines. Search Engine Optimization (SEO) has become the most sought after specialized skill in attracting visitors to companies' websites. The technique is based on understanding how search algorithms work.

The broad basis is optimizing a site's coding presentation and structure and avoiding impediments that might keep search engine-indexing programs from fully detecting a site. It might also involve having unique content on pages that can be easily indexed and extracted by search engines. Since search engine optimization can require making changes to the source code of a site it is beneficial to incorporate this in the initial development and design to make the site 'search engine friendly'.

Because of the specialized skills involved in SEO, if you can afford it, it makes sense to engage the services of professionals to do it for you.

7. Pay per click (PPC) advertising is a good way to target people searching for keywords in your site. Pay per click advertising is advertising in selected search engines. Consumer use of search engines to discover information on products, find local businesses and buy from vendors has never been greater. The ultimate aim of PPC advertising is to appear on the first page of search results and as high up that page as possible. People conducting searches rarely go beyond the first page of search results.

All major search engines such as Google, Yahoo and Bing provide pay-per-click listings, enabling businesses a unique online marketing opportunity. You can easily place limits on spend levels and specify the city, country or countries in which you want the advertisements to appear. As there are strict limits on the number of characters you can include in an ad it is important to carefully research what the key "ad words" are for your site to minimize wastage and to maximize the number of clicks your advertisement receives.

The more you undertake to pay per click the higher your ad will be placed in the search engine results pages. If properly done PPC advertising, provides one of the clearest returns on investment analyses possible from any form of advertising bar none. By individually tracking the effectiveness of each keyword and time of day, as well as the effectiveness of individual creative copy, you will quickly be able to turn PPC search engine advertising into a potent marketing tool.

Search engine advertising represents the most important form of online marketing today. Being immediately and directly responsive to a specific enquiry is the most powerful way to attract prime prospects. Little wonder that search engine advertising is the fastest-growing advertising medium and search engines' advertising revenue is rapidly climbing!

Template 44 - Website promotion strategies (example)	
Product: SoHo modular work stations	
Website promotion checklist	☑ Include web address in all new stationery ☑ Include web address in all sales materials ☑ Include web address in all email signatures ☑ Include web address in all print and advertising materials
Search engine optimization (SEO)	☑ Exchange links with related sites ☑ Submit the site to all major search engines including Google, Yahoo, Bing and AltaVista. ☑ Appoint an SEO specialist to ensure the site is search engine friendly ☑ Include ample high quality content in the site
Search engine advertising	☑ Conduct trials with different keywords in Google's 'AdWords' ☑ Select target markets (countries/regions/cities/languages). ☑ Research and write ad text and select keywords ☑ Set pricing – cost per click and budget per period ☑ Monitor ongoing results from Google Analytics online performance reports and modify strategy accordingly.
Comments: We will constantly monitor Google Analytics to measure and analyze the source of our website traffic and make adjustments as necessary so that the effectiveness of the site is maximized.	

4.8.3 Social Media Marketing

Business class	B2C Products ✔	B2B Products ✔	B2C Services ✔	B2B Services ✔
Plan level	Basic ✔	Intermediate ✔	Advanced ✔	

The phenomenal development of the role of social media in marketing has given rise to an important conduit between marketers and customers. Platforms such as Facebook, Google+, YouTube, Vimeo, Pinterest, Instagram, Snapchat, Twitter and LinkedIn, provide the means by which to conduct exchanges with the public and to create a following that was not previously possible.

It is now possible to have interaction or collaboration with individuals to bridge the gap between the brand and company with customers and prospects to diminish the previous 'unapproachable faceless entity' scenario between companies and customers. Brands that constantly create engaging updates and share important milestones will stay at the forefront of users' attention.

Blogging is an important part of social media marketing particularly when targeting Generations X, Y and Z. In addition to blogging via social media platforms it can be useful to maintain a presence on specialized blog platforms such as WordPress and BlogSpot. Both platforms allow readers to comment and reply.

While increasing your on-line presence, social media lends itself to many forms of content other than text alone. You can upload videos, images and podcasts relevant to your audience. This makes use of social media so valuable in content marketing.

The social media development in marketing is so profound that maintaining a presence on one or more platforms is no longer an option especially given that the only cost is executive time required to consistently update the site. The phenomenon has been accelerated by the amount of time generations 'X' and 'Y' spend on the internet. More and more people are turning to social media for information when making purchasing decisions.

Social media marketing has reached a stage in which in some cases it is not only possible but desirable to concentrate all of an enterprises marketing efforts on this aspect of marketing alone to the exclusion of conventional media. This is particularly applicable to businesses that are entirely or largely reliant on online sales.

Social media marketing programs are usually based on efforts to create content that attracts attention and encourages readers to share it with their social networks. The message spreads from user to user and resonates because people trust personal recommendation or 'word of mouth' more than paid advertising which bombards people thousands of times a day. Stunning results can be achieved if messages 'go viral' reaching a vast audience with surprising impact and immediacy.

The key to successfully promoting products or services in the social media is to choose your platforms carefully so that you most closely match your target market. For example LinkedIn is more relevant for B2B communications while Facebook and Twitter are ideal to reach teenage and young adult consumers.

The second requirement is to provide content that is meaningful so that people actually want to follow you and act positively on the messages communicated.

Another advantage of social media is that you can make special offers or deals for items or discounts of high perceived value that are available on request by email. The resulting response can yield contact details for newsletter databases or to flag special offers and to maintain interaction with customers.

Links to social media platforms from website home pages and vice versa add an extra dimension to customer relationships with brands and manufacturers. It is sound practice to drive people from your website to your social media site and vice versa. Websites can benefit greatly from social media which can deliver mass audiences of relevant users to a site.

Social media marketing should be regarded as part of your overall SEO strategy. A key benefit of leveraging social media is that links are friendly to search engines. They are not purchased or paid links but are automatically driven by users clicking on to your content and linking back to it.

Numbered among social media marketing benefits are:

Provision of a platform to promote a product or service.

Provision of an ability to respond to situations with immediacy and flexibility.

Provision of real time engagement and exchange between the marketer and the public.

Provision of a forum to gauge customer satisfaction or dissatisfaction with a product or service.

Provision of a customer feedback vehicle that identifies customer service improvement opportunities.

Provision of a tool that can be used in the coordination of event management.

Provision of a platform to run promotions and competitions.

Disadvantages include:

Maintenance requires considerable time and effort.

Disgruntled customers or employees can publish negative comments that may not be removable.

Posts are only visible for a short time before they are replaced with newer posts.

Note that social media *marketing* should not be confused with social media *advertising*. Social media marketing is the maintenance of your own presence in social media platforms. Social media advertising is the paid placement of advertisements in social media platforms such as Facebook, YouTube and Twitter in which you can reach specific target markets with far greater accuracy than is possible with conventional mass media advertising.

> "Social media marketing bridges the gap between a company and its customers and prospects"

Template 45 - Social media marketing programs (example)

Product: SoHo work station modules

Platform	Target market	Objectives
Facebook	Small office/home office customers and prospects	1. Interact with users of our products and obtain feedback on their likes and dislikes of their experience with our work station modules. 2. Encourage users to recommend our products to their peers and associates.
Twitter	As above	As above,
LinkedIn	Office furniture retailers	1. Convey positive updates in relation to the progress of the launch program. 2. Persuade non-stockists to stock our products in their stores. 3. Use the site to communicate trade nights and presentations.
YouTube	Small office/home office customers and prospects	Demonstrate SoHo work station modules features and ease of assembly. Embed the video in a prominent place in our website.
Blog platforms	Generations Y & Z	We will maintain a presence on popular blog platforms such as WordPress and BlogSpot.

Comments: We will also consider a presence in Google+ when the above platforms are bedded down and functioning efficiently.

4.9 Merchandising

Business class	B2C Products ✓	B2B Products ✓	B2C Services X	B2B Services X
Plan level	Basic ✓		Intermediate ✓	Advanced ✓

Merchandising is the effort you apply to make your products more prominent and eye catching at point-of-sale. Imaginative merchandising can be very effective in stimulating impulse sales.

Merchandising activities include:
- Influencing the position in-store at which your product is placed.

- Negotiating more display space for your products than competitors' products receive proportionate to sales.
- If your products are displayed in multilevel fixtures (such as in supermarkets) endeavour to negotiate eye level shelf placement.
- Negotiating secondary display sites (off-location displays) at no cost if possible in addition to regular shelving. (Many stores use the demand for in-store 'real estate' as an additional revenue source).
- Drawing attention to your products with special display materials such as posters, show cards, placards, price tickets, elaborate cutouts, showcases and display stands, sample books, customer flyers, videos and corporate brochures.

Many companies go to the extent of employing specialized merchandisers whose primary function is to go from store to store to ensure their companies' products are displayed according to agreed shelf layout schemes and that products are displayed in the most eye catching manner. Merchandisers also physically build large product displays as authorized by the store's head office or store manager.

Some fast moving consumer goods enterprises go to the extent of devising 'plan-o-grams' on behalf of the store chain or group. Plan-o-grams set out recommended shelf layouts for the entire product category including competitors' products. They can ensure that a company's products receive at least proportionate shelf space to market share (but preferably more).

You cannot overestimate the value of your product being shown to advantage in-store as this can provide a significant competitive advantage. It can also lead to valuable impulse sales i.e. sales that were not planned or premeditated by customers.

Unlike many other marketing activities, in-store merchandising is particularly effective because it is directly linked to the product in the location that the product is purchased.

Merchandising can be more effective than expenditure on media advertising for example when customers have to 'bridge the gap' between seeing or hearing the advertised message and the 'place' where the product is available for purchase.

"Imaginative merchandising stimulates impulsive purchasing"

Template 46 - Merchandising program – Year 1. (example)		
Retail Outlet/Store Type	Proposed Merchandising Activity	Proposed Merchandising Materials
Office supply chains (e.g. Officeworks)	Floor stack displays of flat packs where display space is limited. Supplement with show cards and posters showing assembled product	Large strutted show cards. A3 size posters. Flyers for distribution at point-of sale to highlight the modular expansion concept, the locking device feature, the sit/stand feature and product dimension details.
Office furniture retailers	Floor displays of assembled products taking advantage of the eye catching packaging graphics. Supplement displays with quality point of sale materials	Flyers for take home reference
Domestic furniture retailers	As above	As above

"You cannot overestimate the value of your product being shown to advantage in-store"

4.10 Public Relations and Publicity

Business class	B2C Products ✔	B2B Products ✔	B2C Services ✔	B2B Services ✔
Plan level	Basic X		Intermediate ✔	Advanced ✔

Definition: *Public relations is the wide ranging mix of methods and activities employed to establish and promote a favorable relationship with different 'publics' such as consumers, shareholders, employees and government.*

Aspects include press releases, other forms of publicity, seminars, customer functions, special events, corporate entertainment, product launches, government lobbying, community involvement, networking, and sponsorships.

As well as creating favorable publicity, public relations is also sometimes used to minimize or 'hose down' negative publicity.

Publicity is part of the larger concept of public relations involving the process of securing editorial features in print and electronic media where the space (or time) is not paid for. Publicity tends to have more credibility than paid advertising and can be very cost effective as the only costs are those incurred in developing the media releases and in persuading the media to use them.

Public relations consultants are often journalists who have close relationships with the media and have the expertise to 'slant' a media release so that it is suitable for publication.

Publicity is a neglected marketing tool because it is relatively under utilized in relation to other marketing activities. Publicity generally provides more credibility to a product or service than paid advertising because it is compiled (or appears so) by a third party.

The vehicle used to submit items to the media is the media release – a statement prepared by the company or their public relations consultants. The media release sets out the facts and figures of the story and provides contact details for further information.

The main test of media releases suitability for publication is newsworthiness. Products or services that can support stories of interest to readers, listeners, or viewers are those most likely to be used by editors.

Press releases based on mere 'puffery' about products or services are usually not considered suitable for publication.

Some localized or specialized publications can be persuaded to publish editorial articles if press releases are supported with paid advertising.

Many small businesses are able to get articles published in local newspapers, which have less strict guidelines on what constitutes newsworthiness than mainstream media. Published stories are usually more corporate than product oriented. Local sponsorships and 'human interest' stories are often effective in gaining local publicity.

Favorable restaurant reviews are good examples of how publicity can promote a business. Other examples of articles being suitable for press releases are those relating to business awards, human interest stories, situations in which a business creates new employment, achieves an R&D breakthrough or has a community involvement slant.

Whether you're writing a traditional press release, an email or social media pitch, or preparing to make a call to the local media, here are some things to keep in mind:

Quantify interest: Of course your team thinks its interesting news, but will anyone else bat an eyelash? Fine-tune your story — keep the news angle (not you, your company or the product) front and center.

Pick and choose: Keep your personality, do not use jargon and select your words wisely.

Tell a story: Check the five Ws (who, what, when, where and why) off your list, but do it in a compelling format. Don't leave people asking, 'What's the story?' Tell it!

Quotes aren't an afterthought: Don't use quotes to repeat what you've already said; they should amplify your message. And once you're finished, edit down. Fewer words equals a stronger message.

Template 47 - Public relations & publicity activity program (example)

Product:	SoHo work station modules
Program 1 description	Press kit for product launch
Objectives	Gain publicity to create awareness and generate interest in the new range.
Target market	Potential end users and decision makers in the office supply and retail furniture outlets we have targeted.
Proposed media	Specialized office furniture and computer technology magazines.
Format	The kit will include quality photography of the product concept in a work environment situation. The kit will refer to market dynamics which have inspired the product's development, the market gap the range will fill and the unique product features developed for the new product line. Copies of published articles will be sent to potential stockists via a direct mail.
Budget allocated	$5,000
Program 2 description	Trade and media function
Objectives	Gain publicity to create awareness and generate interest in the new range.
Target market	Decision makers in the office supply and retail furniture outlets we have targeted. Specialized office furniture and computer technology magazines journalists
Proposed media	Specialized office furniture and computer technology magazines.
Format	Tied in with the furniture exhibition in which we will participate we will invite key trade customers and trade magazine journalists to an organized launch function at our exhibition stand where they will be able to view assembled samples of the new range. We will provide first class catering, entertainment and door prizes to stimulate interest.
Budget allocated	$16,000

"Publicity generally provides more credibility than paid advertising"

4.11 Sponsorship

Business class	B2C Products ✔	B2B Products ✔	B2C Services ✔	B2B Services ✔
Plan level	Basic ✘	Intermediate ✔		Advanced ✔

Definition: *Sponsorship is the provision of financial support for an event, activity, person or organization or the provision of products or services in return for naming rights and other benefits.* It is usually, but not exclusively, associated with sporting, cultural or community events.

Sponsorships can range from an immense large scale multimillion dollar national basis such as the US Tennis Open and the NFL Super Bowl down to a small scale local community event such as supplying trophies to the local baseball, basketball, tennis or hockey club.

At another level, shoe string budget sponsorship of prizes in kind for local clubs, schools and community groups can generate goodwill and visibility at very low cost such as a local pizza shop donating pizzas as prizes for a school trivia night or a real estate agent sponsoring signage for a church fete.

Sponsors should always ensure that they receive verbal acknowledgement for their involvement in announcements as well as recognition in print materials. Where applicable sponsors should ensure they are given the opportunity to present the sponsored prizes at prize presentation ceremonies.

Sponsorship benefits

Sponsorship of a well-chosen event can enhance the brand or corporate image. For example Coca Cola might sponsor a popular surf carnival or McDonalds might sponsor a children's soccer tournament.

As an added benefit, sponsors often sample or negotiate sole selling rights for their products such as ice cream, snack foods or liquor at sponsored events.

Sponsorships can yield substantial secondary print or electronic media coverage from perimeter signage and other naming rights visibility at sponsored events such as sponsor logos on team uniforms.

Sponsors can make 'community involvement' public relations opportunities available such as in the sponsorship of a local fun run or basketball tournament.

And sponsorships can provide a great platform for high profile customer entertainment and hospitality such as in the sponsorship of a prestigious pro-am golf tournament.

Incremental costs

Before entering into a sponsorships agreement, bear in mind that costs are not limited to the cost of securing sponsorship rights but also involve support costs that can be quite substantial such as signage and printed materials that are essential for involvement recognition. There is also a cost in staffing the sponsorship. These ancillary costs can be as much, or more than the sponsorship naming rights fee.

Some events have many co-sponsors which can mean a significant dilution of visibility. It is therefore important to ensure that the amount of exposure you are given is at least proportionate to the sponsorship fee you have paid.

Template 48 – Proposed sponsorship programs (example)	
Product: SoHo work station modules	
Program description	Co-sponsorship of the 'Small Business of the Year' award at the Furnitex Exhibition
Objectives	Contribute to the development of an awareness profile for the new range.
Target market	Potential end users and decision makers in the office supply and retail furniture outlets we have targeted.
Benefits	We will gain the opportunity to address the audience at the prize presentation ceremony. We will have prominent branding in the competition entry form and other associated literature. We will have access to all the entrants contact details to enable us to conduct email-marketing campaigns targeted to this prime target market.
Budget allocated	The cost will be limited to the donation of a SoHo workstation module to the winner of the award.

"Well-chosen sponsorships can reap significant public relations benefits"

4.12 Corporate Communications

Business class	B2C Products ✔	B2B Products ✔	B2C Services ✔	B2B Services ✔
Plan level	Basic ✔		Intermediate ✔	Advanced ✔

Definition: *The diverse range of essential everyday printed and digital 'sales tools' needed to respond to sales enquiries, use in direct mail campaigns, keep in touch with customers and prospects, and to inform customers, employees and shareholders of developments within your organization.*

Corporate communication items include:
- Corporate brochures
- Corporate or product videos
- Podcasts
- Product catalogues

MARKETING STRATEGIES

- Newsletters
- Sales presenters
- Presentation folders
- Flyers and mailers
- Business cards
- Annual reports
- Portfolios consisting of photos of completed projects and testimonials from satisfied customers.

Many printers offer a complete design service in the production of these materials. There are also many freelance graphic designers and graphic design studios equipped to provide a comprehensive service inclusive of copywriting, design, photography, artwork, pre-press and printing supervision.

Corporate communication materials do not have to be elaborate or expensive to produce. For example a small garden landscape business might keep a photographic portfolio of completed jobs to present to prospective customers.

A supply of selected multipurpose corporate communication materials is a basic part of most firm's sales and marketing requirements although hard copy materials are giving way to electronic communications materials such as pdf's (portable document formats) which can be quickly and cheaply sent to contacts via email.

Template 49 - Corporate communications materials program (example)

Product: SoHo work station modules

Item	Communications objectives	Target market
Glossy product brochure in hard copy and pdf formats	For use as a sales presenter to assist in gaining retail trade orders	Office furniture retailers
Product flyers for use as a handout at point-of-sale, and trade exhibitions and as a utility mailer.	To provide potential customers with detailed product information including product specifications.	Prospective end users
Video for screening at trade exhibitions, in-store displays and the corporate website.	Demonstrate benefits such as ease of assembly and functionality	Prospective end users and retail trade buyers.

"A select range of corporate communications 'sales tools' is essential for every business"

4.13 Direct Marketing and Database Marketing

Business class	B2C Products ✓	B2B Products ✓	B2C Services ✓	B2B Services ✓
Plan level	Basic ✓	Intermediate ✓		Advanced ✓

Direct Marketing is a branch of marketing that communicates directly to target markets via 'addressable media' such as mail, telemarketing and email. It differs from advertising in that it does not communicate via third party media such as TV, radio and print.

Database marketing is an evolutionary refinement of direct marketing using computer databases that are continually updated with customers and prospects records such as buying history, demographics, personal preferences and so forth. It is most effective when used as an ongoing process in emailing newsletters and other forms of communications. It is a powerful, more targeted cost effective tool compared with mass media, which have immense wastage.

The main benefit of database marketing is the ability to target your marketing and promotional programs to prime prospects unlike other media, which are difficult to assess since there is no direct response from the consumer. With database marketing you can measure the results and continue to refine your tactics and strategies.

You can also personalise your communications and even vary the message according to different sub-sectors of the target group.

The main forms of direct marketing are:
→ Direct mail
→ Letter box drops
→ Mass email campaigns (email marketing)
→ Text messages via SMS
→ Telemarketing
→ Telephone messaging

Direct mail allows the marketer to design mailers in many different formats. Some of these are catalogues, self-mailers (a folded item that requires no envelope), postcards, and dimensional mailers (in many different shapes and sizes). Within these and other formats, there is ample scope to use creativity to get the recipient's attention.

Disadvantages of direct mail include wastage resulting from the 'junk mail' reputation when overused, labor intensiveness in sorting and handling and the high cost of postage in some countries.

Letterbox drops (in which unaddressed leaflets or flyers are delivered directly to householders or businesses) are an offshoot of direct mail suitable for small localized businesses such as retailers and tradesmen for example plumbers, hairdressers, painters, electricians, garden maintenance contractors, pool cleaning services, security products and handymen. You can engage the services of letterbox distribution companies to physically 'drop' the sales material into household or business letterboxes in carefully selected post or zip codes.

Alternatively if you are on a shoestring budget you could 'do it yourself'. One of the great advantages of letterbox drops is the relative ease of measuring response rates if this is the only form of 'advertising' in which you are participating. It is often an underrated cost effective option.

Mass email marketing has soared in popularity and is effective where databases with recipient permissions are maintained. Email messages are often designed in the same html format (Hyper Text Markup Language) as web pages with links to the marketer's website. Common users of mass email are companies with strategies designed to maintain relationships with existing customers, shareholders, club members and the like. Other users of mass email are operators of loyalty programs such as those used by airlines, supermarket chains, book stores, car dealers, and travel agents. Companies that sell direct to the public can use the medium very effectively.

Mass email marketing is the Internet's version of direct mail. It is the fastest growing form of database marketing as today's computer database and spreadsheet programs have simplified the process so that it is low cost and can be generated quickly.

This type of customer communication can have the added benefit of real time reports provided by mass email platforms which provide feedback on emails sent that were opened, clicked through, bounced, sent to friends or unsubscribed.

Sending emails to people without their consent is known as 'spamming' and is illegal in some countries. For this reason marketers usually generate their databases by asking customers' and prospects' permission when they are purchasing a product or service, entering a competition or other promotion or express interest in receiving special offers or updates from a facility in the marketer's website (on-line registration). Even then it is necessary to give people an 'unsubscribe' option each time a communication is addressed to them.

Database Building Strategies

1. Include a newsletter subscription link to a web form on your website home page.

2. Add a newsletter subscription link to a web form in email signatures.

3. Draw attention to the newsletter and invite people to register to receive future issues in business stationery and corporate brochures.

4. Refer to the newsletter in sales calls with existing customers and prospects. Ask them if they would like to receive future issues.

5. Collect email addresses from customers and prospects business cards exchanged in the normal course of business and add them to the database.

6. Give contacts a reason to receive the newsletter such as "get all the latest industry news and information with helpful tips and advice" or "receive discounts and special offers".

Telemarketing

In telemarketing, as the name suggests, marketers contact customers and prospects via telephone usually from a specially set-up call center. One of the attractions of telemarketing is the speed with which campaigns can be executed. While direct mail can be cost-effective, it is relatively slower than telemarketing because of the logistics involved. Telemarketing also lends itself to products and services that are complex to buy, promote a financial service or to solicit donations to charities. Telemarketing allows a company representative to use persuasion and to explain any complexities.

Telemarketing can take two main forms.

- Outbound telemarketing: Through using auto dialers and predictive dialers, call centers can call a large number of customers in a short period of time.
- Inbound telemarketing: Promotions and offers made when a customer calls the center in response to other advertising.

One of the disadvantages of telemarketing is a negative consumer attitude to this form of unsolicited promotion, which are often regarded unfavorably as 'nuisance calls'.

SMS Telephone messaging

This is similar to mass emailing using mobile phone technology to send SMS messages to consumers from a central database. It is a growing emerging direct marketing technique that has accelerated since the rollout of 4G and higher technology.

Emerging channels

Pay TV is being promoted as the technology solution of the future that will deliver increasing direct response opportunities via television.

Direct response

A related form of marketing is direct response marketing. In direct marketing, the marketer contacts the potential customer directly, but in direct response marketing the customer responds to the marketer directly. Its most common form today is via TV infomercials in which consumers respond via telephone or internet with credit card in hand. Other media, such as magazines, newspapers, radio, and email can be used to obtain the response, but tend to achieve lower response rates than television.

Direct and database marketing is often carried out by specialist service providers. The services provided by these companies includes the maintenance of mailing lists and the production of mailing pieces.

"Database marketing can target your prime prospects more accurately than any other media"

Template 50 - Direct marketing & database marketing programs

Product: SoHo work station modules

Program	Communications objectives	Target market
Mass email marketing	'Up sell' and 'cross sell' Communicate work station modules innovations and benefits	Small office and home office purchasers and potential purchasers
Direct mail	Pre-sell the concept prior to sales reps initial sales call.	Targeted retail stockists
Telesales	Promote awareness of the product line and to schedule sales call appointments and monitor retail stock levels	Retail buyers and store managers.

"Building and maintaining accurate up-to-date databases of customers and prospects is a valuable marketing asset"

CHAPTER 5. FINANCIAL STATEMENTS
5.1 Marketing Budget

Business class	B2C Products ✔	B2B Products ✔	B2C Services ✔	B2B Services ✔
Plan level	Basic ✔	Intermediate ✔		Advanced ✔

Framing the marketing budget is a complex and painstaking exercise as there is no standard formula. The amount spent on marketing proportionate to revenue varies considerably from one industry and set of circumstances to another.

Marketing budgets vary from around 1% of gross revenue for B2B businesses to about 20% for B2C operations. Fast moving consumer goods companies (such as Procter & Gamble) traditionally spend around 10% of sales on advertising alone. High profile retail chains often spend as much as 20% of gross revenue. Depending on profit margins the cost of launching new products can be as much as 50% of gross revenue in the first year before settling down to a more sustainable level.

Some of the more usual approaches are:

- Start with a "wish list" of all the things you think would achieve your goals. This could be broken down by 'need to do' and 'like to do'. When you have added up the aggregate cost you can start to eliminate the 'like to do' items on a prioritized basis.
- Allocating a fixed percentage of sales on a calendar or financial year basis referenced by historical levels.
- Estimating what it would cost on a budget line-by-line basis to reach your sales and profit goals.
- Estimating how much your competitors spend on marketing, then allocating a proportionate amount based on relative market share.
- Allocating a figure your company can reasonably afford before determining what you can purchase with the allocated funds.
- Determining the level of investment that is acceptable in the overall corporate budget.
- A combination of all of the above overlaid with good old fashioned business judgement.

It is more effective to concentrate the budget on a few carefully selected high priority items (and do them well) than to attempt to spread the same level of aggregate spend over too many items (and do nothing adequately) in an attempt to 'cover all the bases'.

Once the total amount is set the budget should be itemized by product/item/time frame.

The practicality of the budget when set should be assessed in the financial statement in terms of its 'fit' with corporate goals and objectives.

Marketing budgets normally comprise only direct costs. Indirect costs such as wages and salaries and other overheads are not part of this budget.

Many businesses fail because they do not allocate sufficient funds for marketing and cut budgets when encountering difficult market conditions. When the market is tough you need to hold your nerve. It is difficult, if not impossible, to grow businesses without adequate marketing funding.

Template 51 - Marketing budget: Year 1 (example)

Item	Budget $	Item	Budget $	Item	Budget $
MEDIA ADVERTISING		PRINT		OTHER	
TV & radio	-	Corporate brochures & flyers	20,000	Public relations & publicity	5,000
Newspapers & magazines	35,000	Sales presenters	10,000	Trade functions	16,000
Cooperative trade advertising	40,000	Product catalogues	30,000	Marketing research	10,000
Social media advertising	3,000	Merchandising & display materials	40,000	Showroom upgrade	50,000
Directory advertising	1,000			Packaging materials design	5,000
Media production costs	5,000			Product development	30,000
Ad agency & consultants fees	7,000			Sponsorships	2,000
Other	-			Signage	10,000
SUB TOTAL	91,000	SUB TOTAL	100,000	SUB TOTAL	128,000
PROMOTIONS		ONLINE MARKETING		CONTINGENCY	
Sales promotions - consumer	-	Website development & maintenance	20,000	Contingency for unplanned items	39,000
Sales promotions – trade	20,000	Search engine advertising	10,000		
Sales incentive schemes	25,000	Search engine optimization (SEO)	2,000		
Trade shows & exhibitions	15,000	Database marketing	4,000		
Promotional videos & DVD's	10,000	Social media marketing	1,000		
Direct marketing	10,000				
Promotional merchandise	5,000				
SUB TOTAL	85,000	SUB TOTAL	37,000	TOTAL MARKETING BUDGET	$480,000

NOTE: This list is not intended to be a comprehensive list of marketing budget items. Your business may use some of these categories and others not included above that are specific to your business category.

5.2 Marketing Financial Statement

Business class	B2C Products ✓	B2B Products ✓	B2C Services ✓	B2B Services ✓
Plan level	Basic ✓		Intermediate ✓	Advanced ✓

The marketing plan would not be complete without a financial statement setting out forecast revenue, marketing and other costs and overheads and projected profit levels and margins.

This is an examination of the fiscal practicality of the marketing plan and its ability to meet corporate expectations.

To gain an indication of the degree of risk in the plan it is advisable to base projections on three levels – 'pessimistic', 'optimistic' with 'most likely' in the middle of the range.

Although the plan is for an initial twelve month period, the financial statement should ideally include an indicative outlook for the next two years showing anticipated trends in revenue, direct costs, expenses and overheads and profit.

Depending on the degree of investment in the plan in some cases it might be acceptable to set 'break even' or even negative returns for a predetermined period. This scenario would be more likely when the plan is based on the development of a new product or a new product range where the costs of development could be borne by established 'cash cows' in the company's product portfolio.

It is important that projections are accurate and realistic. If launching a new product do not underestimate initial financial requirements. It is prudent to err on the conservative side when forecasting sales and on the high side when estimating expenses.

As the financial statement is the ultimate indicator of the desired outcomes of the plan, the degree of risk involved needs to be clearly quantified and understood.

The financial statement can be in respect of a single product or a group of products marketed under the same brand. The latter is particularly appropriate when you want to measure the overall effect of the launch of a new product on the sales and profitability of existing products.

The financial statement opposite is representative of the latter. Note that other accounting/financial models to that shown are equally acceptable providing sales forecasts and marketing and other costs are reflected in the statement to show a scenario of likely outcomes.

It is prudent to err on the conservative side when forecasting sales and on the high side when estimating costs

Template 52 - Marketing financial statement: Years 1 to 3 (example)

$000's	Year 1			Year 2			Year 3		
	Pessimistic	Most Likely	Optimistic	Pessimistic	Most Likely	Optimistic	Pessimistic	Most Likely	Optimistic
SALES									
Product 1 - Desks	630	700	770	570	630	690	510	560	625
Product 2 – Returns	180	200	220	160	180	200	145	160	180
Product 3 – Screens	90	100	110	80	90	100	73	85	90
Product 4 – Work stations	280	300	320	500	600	650	900	1095	1195
TOTAL REVENUE	1,180	1,300	1,420	1,310	1,500	1,640	1,628	1,900	2,090
Direct costs									
Product 1 - Desks	158	175	192	145	157	170	131	140	156
Product 2 - Returns	45	50	55	40	45	50	36	40	45
Product 3 - Screens	22	25	28	20	23	25	18	20	24
Product 4 – Work stations	70	75	80	125	150	165	225	275	300
TOTAL DIRECT COSTS	295	325	355	330	375	410	410	475	525
Gross margin	885	975	1,065	980	1,125	1,230	1,218	1,425	1,565
% of sales	75	75	75	75	75	75	75	75	75
LESS OPERATING COSTS									
Marketing	480	480	480	515	515	515	550	550	550
% of sales	41	37	34	39	34	31	34	29	26
Admin & overheads	240	240	240	250	250	250	260	260	260
% of sales	20	18	17	19	17	15	16	14	12
TOTAL OPERATING COSTS	720	720	720	765	765	765	810	810	810
% of sales	61	55	51	58	51	47	50	43	39
EARNING BEFORE INTEREST & TAX (EBIT)	165	255	345	215	360	465	408	615	755
% of sales	14	20	24	16	24	28	25	32	36

KEY POINTS: Based on the 'Most Likely' scenario, the planned financial result is to accept a short term loss from the new product range in the development stage when earnings before interest and tax (EBIT), subsidized by existing products, is forecast at $255,000 from revenue of $1.3 million in year 1. This will grow to an EBIT of around $615,000 from $1.9 million in revenue in year 3 when the company will be better placed to sustain long term growth.

CHAPTER 6. IMPLEMENTATION AND CONTROLS
6.1 Sales & Marketing Personnel Resources

Business class	B2C Products ✔	B2B Products ✔	B2C Services ✔	B2B Services ✔
Plan level	Basic ✘	Intermediate ✔		Advanced ✔

This part of the plan addresses the personnel resources you will have in place to implement the plan. As this is a marketing plan this section is confined to sales and marketing employees and does not address administration, production and other departments.

In most small enterprises the entire sales and marketing function (along with a host of other responsibilities) will be handled by the business owner or general manager. Larger businesses might split the two functions while others will outsource some of the functions to marketing consultants and other specialists such as merchandisers, graphic and web designers.

Some medium enterprises at the upper end of the scale (anything up to 100 employees) might structure a marketing department with brand or product managers and other specialists. However the trend is towards keeping fixed overheads to a minimum and to outsource specialist services as required.

Regardless of whether personnel have a direct sales or marketing responsibility or not it is important to cultivate a marketing and customer service mind-set among everyone employed in the business from warehouse employees to delivery drivers and office personnel.

For example the company receptionist is a key part of the marketing function as she creates the first impression among customers and prospects and her product knowledge and marketing mind-set can positively influence sales enquiries considerably.

Marketing orientation can be encouraged by involving employees in the planning process and briefing them on the details and progress of the plan. You should encourage them to have a sound knowledge of your products and services and to be on the lookout and report on competitor activity and sales opportunities. A bonus or reward system will provide incentives for this.

As a general policy it is always beneficial to employ the most highly skilled people you can find and to train them on new developments and skills by running internal training courses and sending them to selected external courses. This will not only increase the collective skills of the organization but will also raise the level of commitment to the business.

One of the keys to running a successful sales and marketing function is to ensure everyone knows exactly what their responsibilities are and what they are expected to achieve. Drawing up an organisational chart is a good way to define everyone's reporting links and overall areas of responsibility.

Clear job descriptions are a part of this process along with including an action timetable in the plan showing who is responsible for each task and the date each assignment is expected to be complete.

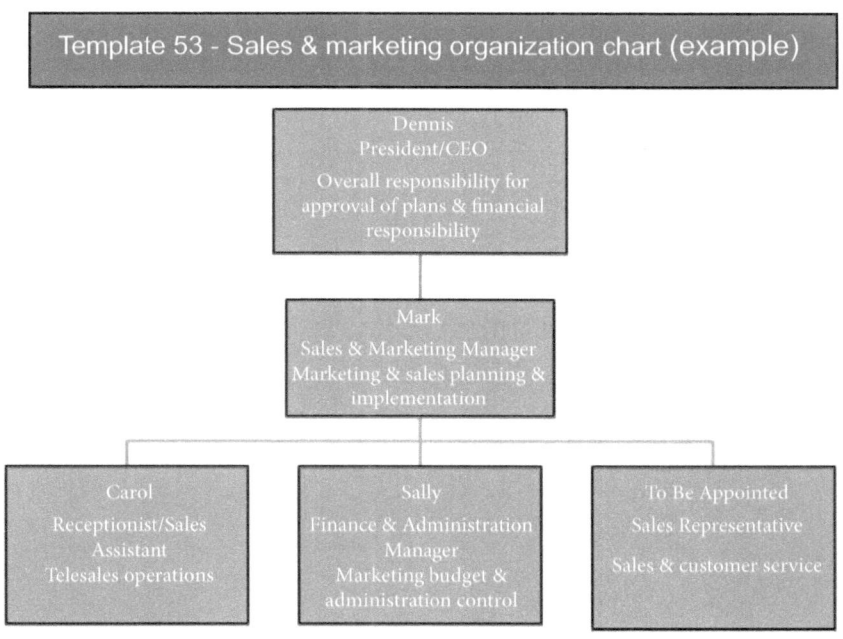

"Every plan should be clear on accountability"

6.2 Action Plan

Business class	B2C Products ✔	B2B Products ✔	B2C Services ✔	B2B Services ✔
Plan level	Basic ✔	Intermediate ✔		Advanced ✔

There are five steps to setting the action plan and timetable:
1. State the activity
2. Define the action steps. The more definitive they are the better as they can be more easily monitored.
3. Assign a target date for completing the activity
4. Assign responsibility to a single person
5. Record the results to track progress and for future use.

This simple process clarifies 'who is responsible for what and when' and provides accountability to the plan.

A separate action plan should be prepared for each phase of the plan.

Template 54 - Action plan stage 1. Pre-launch phase (example)

Development stage	Action steps	Target completion date	Person responsible	Results achieved
Market research	Qualitative consumer concept product research	Completed	Mark	Positive consumer demand confirmed. Improvements identified.
	Test reaction to prototype among target market	July 2017	Mark	Excellent responses received to date.
Product development	Research global development in work station modules	July 2017	Mark	Some good ideas identified from web research
	Finalize product design & specifications	September 2017	Mark & Dennis	Preliminary designs look promising
	Product prototype	October 2017	Dennis	Produced on schedule
	Commence commercial production	January 2018	Dennis	On schedule
Packaging development	Commence flat pack design and specifications with packaging supplier	October 2017	Dennis & Dennis	On schedule
	Brief graphic designer for flat pack graphics design including essential text such as assembly instructions	October 2017	Mark	On schedule

6.3 Implementation Schedule

Business class	B2C Products ✓	B2B Products ✓	B2C Services ✓	B2B Services ✓
Plan level	Basic ✓	Intermediate ✓	Advanced ✓	

The implementation schedule is a graphic representation of the plan that sets out the sequential and overlapping timing of the different components parts.

The aim is to ensure that each component part is completed in time for the implementation of the next part of the plan.

The component parts will vary from one plan to another according to whether the plan is for new or existing products or services and the degree of complexity.

The more detail you include the better. Progress should be monitored on a regular basis and updated as implementation of the plan progresses.

"The implementation schedule ensures that all the parts of the plan come together in the right sequence"

Template 55 – Implementation schedule (example)

Plan Stage	Timing																			
Month	M	J	J	A	S	O	N	D	J	F	M	A	M	J	J	A	S	O	N	D
Product development	▮	▮																		
Product design		▮	▮																	
Commercial factory production				▮	▮	▮	▮	▮	▮	▮										
Market research				▮																
Launch selling materials							▮	▮												
Product sell-in										▮	▮									
Distribution rollout											▮	▮	▮							
Advertising														▮	▮	▮				
Promotions											▮	▮						▮	▮	
Merchandising																	▮	▮		
(Add other stages as required)																				
	Year 1								Year 2											

NOTE: These steps are indicative only and should be modified to meet the primary stages of each individual plan.

6.4 Review & Evaluation Schedule

Business class	B2C Products ✔	B2B Products ✔	B2C Services ✔	B2B Services ✔
Plan level	Basic X		Intermediate ✔	Advanced ✔

Fine tuning and even implementing major changes in direction is sometimes necessary to accommodate changing circumstances and market conditions.

This schedule reviews the steps you have taken after a specified period (usually a year). It evaluates progress, estimates effectiveness and suggests any changes based on your experience to date.

Effectiveness should be based on a measured assessment against clear objectives that were set for the activity in the first place. If not possible to quantify results a subjective assessment will suffice providing it reflects a range of views and opinions.

The evaluation should recognize the adequateness of time given to date and the resources allocated to the activity thus far.

Proposed changes should be incorporated in a plan update of at least the templates affected.

"You should always track results achieved against the set targets"

Template 55 – Review & evaluation schedule (example)

Plan Stage	Progress Evaluation	Effectiveness (1 – 10)	Proposed Changes	For action by
Product development	Outstanding concept developed	9	Modifications required to locking device	Dennis
Product design completion	Designs completed on time and on budget	8	Modifications to desking screens required	Dennis
Commercial Production	Excellent quality. Need more flexibility to meet immediate orders	8	We need some adjustments to factory stock levels	Dennis
Market Research	Need more info on price elasticity	8	Implement a study among initial purchasers to include price reaction	Mark
Launch materials	On time and on budget. Worked well	9	No further action required	N/A
Product sell in	On schedule. Could have done better detailing concept to retail sales people	7	Need to start planning for expansion into other markets	Mark
Distribution	Mostly on schedule. Missed a couple of important deadlines	6	Need to review further stockists opportunities	Mark
Advertising	Seems to be working well. Retailers like it.	8	More of the same for now	Mark
Promotions	Budget for temporary price reductions overspent but concept worked well	6	Need tighter controls to monitor allowances for temporary price reductions	Mark
Merchandising	Only 65% of targeted in-store displays achieved in first year	6	Consider engaging a part time merchandiser to assemble and erect displays in accordance with agreements reached with store managers.	Mark

Executive Summary

Business class	B2C Products ✓	B2B Products ✓	B2C Services ✓	B2B Services ✓
Plan level	Basic ✓		Intermediate ✓	Advanced ✓

The purpose of the executive summary is to provide the reader with an overview explaining where your business has been and where it is going as a result of the strategies developed in the plan.

Although the executive summary appears at the start of the completed plan, it can only be written when the rest of the plan is in place. Use the headings below as a checklist. Add subject matter that is relevant to your business and project.

Template 57 - Executive summary (example)

When and why the business was established	Established in 1980 manufacturing a range of traditional executive office desks and other office furniture.
Geographical markets it was set up to cover.	San Diego and surrounding counties
A description of the products we offer	Traditional office desks, returns and screens as well as complimentary bookcases, office chairs, tables and filing cabinets.
Trade customers profile	Office furniture retailers, domestic furniture retailers and office supply chains.
End user customers profile	Small to medium corporate offices (until now). This will be redirected to operators working from small offices/home offices
A summary of our progress in the market to date	Turnover increased at a rate of 10% in first twenty years but has since leveled out at around $1Million per annum.
The dynamics that have arisen that need to be addressed	Our current product base is being eroded. Trend away from traditional office furniture to more space efficient workstations. Also cheaper imports presenting increasing threat.
The main factors that will lead to forecast sales and profits	We have identified a breakthrough opportunity in a plan to enter the less competitive but growing small office/home office market segments with a specialized line of high-end workstation modules. This new product introduction will be supported with carefully devised strategies in a coordinated marketing plan that will change our thinking from production to consumer driven orientation.
The impact the plan will have on revenue and profit.	The planned financial result is to accept a short-term loss from the new product range in the development stage when Earnings Before Interest and Tax (EBIT), subsidized by existing products, is forecast at $255,000 from revenue of $1.3M in year 1. This will grow to around an EBIT of $615,000 from $1.9M in revenue in year 3 when the company will be better placed to sustain long-term growth.

APPENDIX
CONSOLIDATED SAMPLE MARKETING PLAN

Wellbuilt Furniture Inc.

Marketing Plan for New Product Line Introduction

SoHo Work Station Modules
for the
Small office/Home Office

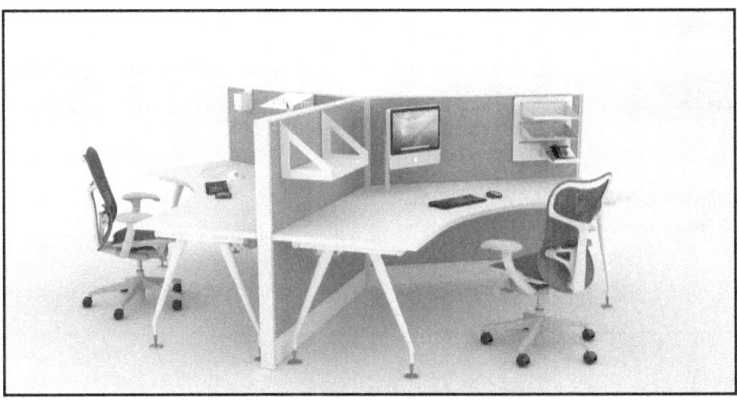

Prepared by: Mark Miller, Sales & Marketing Manager

March 2018

Note: This marketing plan is based on a fictitious office furniture manufacturing company. Any resemblance between the business depicted and any actual business is entirely coincidental.

Executive Summary	
When and why the business was established.	Established in 1980 manufacturing a range of traditional executive office desks and other office furniture.
Geographical markets it was set up to cover.	San Diego and surrounding counties
A description of the current products we offer	Traditional office desks returns and screens as well as complimentary bookcases, office chairs, tables and filing cabinets.
Trade customers profile	Office furniture retailers, domestic furniture retailers and office supply chains.
End user customers profile	(Until now) small to medium corporate offices. This will be redirected to people working from small offices/home offices
A summary of our progress in the market to date	Turnover grew at a rate of 10% in first twenty years but has leveled out at around $1Million per annum.
The dynamics that have arisen that need to be addressed	Our current product base is being eroded. Trend away from traditional office furniture to more space efficient workstations. Also cheap imports presenting increasing threat.
The main factors that will lead to forecast sales and profits	We have identified a breakthrough opportunity in a plan to enter the less competitive but growing small office/home office market segments with a specialized line of high end work station modules. This new product introduction will be supported with carefully devised strategies in a coordinated marketing plan that will change our thinking from production to consumer driven orientation.
The impact the plan will have on revenue and profit.	The planned financial result is to accept a short-term loss from the new product line in the development stage when earnings before interest and tax (EBIT), subsidized by existing products, is forecast at $155,000 from revenue of $1.3M in year 1. This will grow to an EBIT of around $535,000 from $1.9M in revenue in year 3 when the company will be better placed to sustain long-term growth.

PART 1: SALES & MARKET REVIEW
1.1 Sales analysis

	Existing Products Sales Analysis									
	Turnover $000s			Gross Profit or Loss $000s			Net Profit or loss $000s		
Product or Service	3 years ago	2 years ago	Last year	3 years ago	2 years ago	Last year	3 years ago	2 years ago	Last year
Executive desks, returns & Screens	1,300	1,200	1,100	715	660	605	286	264	242
Bookcases	110	105	100	55	50	45	22	21	20
Office chairs	210	200	190	105	100	95	42	40	35
Office tables	300	290	280	150	145	140	60	55	50
Filing cabinets	150	140	150	30	28	30	(15)	(14)	(15)
Total	2,070	1,935	1,820	1,055	983	915	395	366	332
Conclusion: Sales of our entire product range are flat or in decline. We need to develop new products for future sustainable growth as a matter of urgent priority!									

KEY POINTS:

A sales analysis of our product portfolio has shown that in the last three years:
1. Executive desks returns and screens have been in slow decline in turnover and in both gross and net profit.
2. All other products are falling in all three measures.
3. On a consolidated basis turnover and profit is falling with the implication that if we are not proactive in changing our marketing strategy and product mix, the future viability of the business is problematic.

1.2 Products & services review

Existing Products or Services Review				
Product or Service	Benefits	Comparison with competitors	Profit contributor Rating (1 – 10)	Product or service classification
Executive desks, returns & Screens	High quality craftsmanship	Better built than most	10	Cash cow but under threat
Bookcases	Easily assembled	Middle quality range	5	Future questionable
Office chairs	Gas lifts	No clear advantage	4	Limited growth opportunity
Office tables	Solid timber	High quality end	6	Cash cow but slowing demand
Filing cabinets	Fully welded	In most expensive quartile	3	Losing money but completes a range

KEY POINTS:

In a Boston Consulting Group matrix analysis based on the above sales analysis we have also established:

1. There are no 'rising stars' in our current product portfolio.
2. Our only 'cash cow' is executive desks. Fortunately this will provide the funds required for product and market development.
3. Bookcases, office chairs and tables are 'question marks'
4. Filing cabinets are rated as 'dogs' given that they are incurring losses and are therefore earmarked to be deleted from the range.

We have concluded that all our existing products are in a mature stage or under threat with the clear implication that new product development is imperative if the business is to survive let alone thrive in the future.

1.3 Market segmentation

We have segmented the office furniture market into four primary groups as follows:

Market Segments	
Large office fit outs	**Large office replacements and additions**
New and refurbished buildings – usually specified by architect or other – purchases direct from manufacturer.	Existing workplaces – purchase from manufacturers direct or from wholesalers or specialist office furniture retailers.
Small offices	**Home offices**
Fewer than 12 people. Usually purchase from specialist office furniture retailers.	One or two person offices. Usually purchase from general furniture retailers with a limited office furniture section.

As shown in the table below, we have further determined which of the four market segments hold the most potential for development by our company in terms of competitor servicing, our potential ability to service, estimated growth rates and our levels of priority.

Market segmentation and opportunity rating				
Existing & Potential market segments	Rate the extent to which the segment is already being serviced by competitors Scale 1-10	Rate your current or potential ability to service this segment Scale 1-10	Estimated growth rate Scale 1-10	Rate your level of priority Scale 1-10
Large office fit outs	10	0	4	0
Large office replacements	7	2	3	3
Small offices	3	8	9	10
Home offices	2	10	9	10
Conclusion: Large office fit outs and replacements are already dominated by the large commercial furniture manufacturers. Based on existing competition, our ability to service and estimated growth rates, the small office/home office segments are the segments with the best potential in which to concentrate our resources.				

1.4 Product segmentation
1.4.1 Product segmentation by size and trend

The office furniture market is broken down into six primary product segments as shown below. Due to market shifts there has been a trend towards large companies outsourcing services to businesses operating from small and home offices where office space is very limited. Consequently, demand is rapidly growing for highly efficient space economic work stations. We believe we have identified an untapped market opportunity to focus on high end work station modules for small offices/home offices.

Market breakdown by product segmentation				
Product segment	Product segment volume Units	Product segment value $	Estimated product share of market by value %	Life cycle stage Growth, maturity or decline
1. Work stations	25,000	$50M	26	Rapid Growth
2. Desks	30,000	$75M	39	Mature
3. Returns	5,000	$12M	6	Slow decline
4. Work tables	19,000	$45M	22	Slow Decline
5. Storage units	3,000	$7M	4	Slow Decline
6. Screens	2,000	$5	3	Slow Decline
TOTAL MARKET	84,000	$194M	100	
KEY POINTS: 1. Corporate offices are down sizing due to technology advancements, office rent and labor costs which are influencing a trend away from office desks to workstations. 2. Work stations product segment has grown to become the second largest segment by volume and value. It is the only segment in a rapid growth phase as a result of the changing market dynamics.				

1.4.2 Product segments by channels of distribution

Product segments by channels of distribution						
Market segment: Small offices/ home offices	Channels of distribution %					
Product segment	Channel 1. Direct from factory	Channel 2. Office furniture manufacturers	Channel 3. Domestic furniture manufacturers	Channel 4. Office Supply Chains	Channel 5. Wholesalers	Channel 6. eCommerce
1. Work stations	10	45	25	12	8	0
2. Desks	20	35	30	10	3	2
3. Returns	20	35	30	10	3	2
4. Work tables	25	35	25	10	3	2
5. Storage units	25	35	25	10	3	2
6. Screens	25	35	25	10	32	
KEY POINT: Unlike large and medium offices whose office furniture needs are primarily serviced direct from manufacturers, the majority of small office/home office furniture needs are purchased retail.						

1.5 Competitor analysis

Criteria	Our company: Wellbuilt	Competitor 1 Name: Premier	Competitor 2 Name Stylecraft	Competitor 3 Name: Colonial	Competitor 4 Name: Nova
Estimated market share	Around 8%	45%	20%	10%	5%
Estimated annual sales	$1,200,000	$7,000,000	$3,000,000	$1,500,000	$700,000
Reputation in market	High end	The industry standard	Solid	Not well defined	Cheap
Price	Premium	High end	Medium to high	Middle range	Low end
Product quality	High	Medium to high	Middle range	Average	Poor
Product range	Comprehensive	Comprehensive	Comprehensive	Limited	Basic
Service	Fair	Excellent	Good	Good	Poor
Location	Prime position to service local market	Central	Acceptable	Acceptable	Poor
Distribution	Patchy	Extensive	Fair	Selective	Poor
Advertising	Limited at present	Prominent	Prominent in local press	None that we can discern	None
Innovation	Lacking to date	Leaders	Usually follow Bettabilt	Nothing to go on recently	Just copies others
Current market segment focus	Large office ad hoc replacement and additions	Large office fit outs and large office ad hoc replacements and additions	Large office ad hoc replacement and additions	Large office ad hoc replacement and additions	Large office ad hoc replacement and additions

KEY POINTS: Based on the competitor analysis above, the reality is that we are currently a small fish in a big pond. Furthermore our share of that pond is contracting due to changing market dynamics. Fortunately, we have identified an underdeveloped market segment in which our competitive position would be that of a bigger fish in a small but growing pond. Our competitive position will be greatly advantaged if we are "first in" to gain leadership of this market segment in our traditional home base.

1.6 Marketing research

Product concept marketing research checklist	
Product concept	High quality/high tech, space efficient, extendable work stations
Market segment	Small offices and home offices
Research objective	Test the validity and the extent to which these market segments offer a viable market opportunity
What we need to know	
Existing behavior	What office furniture equipment are they using now?
Satisfaction with existing products	The extent to which the target market is satisfied/not satisfied with office furniture currently available?
Product needs	What features does the target market require?
Where do they purchase?	Direct from manufacturer? Office furniture retailers? Domestic furniture retailers? Office supplies stores?
How frequently do they purchase?	Once a year? Every two years? On a needs basis only?
What would influence brand or products switching?	Better functionality? More efficient use of available floor space? Better value for money? Other?
How much are they prepared to pay?	Under $500 per work station. $501 to $750. $751 to $1,000. $1,000 plus.

Comment: Before committing to the proposed change in market focus, we have identified the fundamental things we need to know (as shown above) to assist us in formulating our marketing strategies. We will commission a small-scale qualitative research study conducted by a specialized research organization to hopefully validate the viability of the proposed product concept.

PART 2 SITUATION ANALYSIS
2.1 SWOT analysis

SWOT Analysis

STRENGTHS (Internal)
1. Excellent product quality and design capability.
2. A growing understanding and appreciation of market dynamics.
3. Good liquidity and debt free as a result of sound financial management.
4. Ample production capacity.
5. A stable and skilled workforce.

WEAKNESSES (internal)
1. Static sales of existing products in a mature market.
2. No significant growth prospects on the horizon in existing product class.
3. Virtually no marketing programs in place at present.
4. Distribution limited to too few outlets making us vulnerable to deletion and diminishing market presence.

OPPORTUNITIES (external)
1. Strong growth in demand for furniture for small and home offices such as high end work stations.
2. These market segments are not dominated by existing suppliers.
3. Finance is available for expansion if needed.
4. Internet marketing offers potential.

THREATS (external)
1. Imports of standard office furniture products are growing.
2. Increasing competition as other small furniture manufacturers are constantly entering the office furniture segment.
3. Large and small end users are replacing conventional desks with more efficient workstations.

KEY LEVERAGE POINTS
We need to leverage our production and design strengths and harness our financial resources to establish a commanding presence in a growing market segment niche not yet universally identified by existing large competitors.

BUSINESS IMPLICATIONS
1. We need to be less vulnerable to imports and to target our market more effectively.
2. We also need to change our focus from a declining highly competitive market to one that is growing and is less vulnerable to competition.

SUSTAINABLE COMPETITIVE ADVANTAGES

We have the ability to capitalize on our established production strengths coupled with our acquired marketing orientation to recognize and target more potentially rewarding and less competitive new product market segments such as specialized work stations for small and home offices.

2.2 Mission statement

Mission statement components	
Business we are in	State-of-the-art equipment for small and home offices
The products we produce	State of the art work station furniture
The customers we serve	People working from small offices/home offices and who are early adopters of developments in office technology
The area we serve	The city and surrounding districts of San Diego CA
The benefits to customers	Efficient, comfortable and flexible work station furniture that creates an environment for improved functionality and productivity in less work space
The benefits to the community	Being a responsible employer and supporter of local community affairs
The benefits to our employees	Fair compensation for effort in a secure, stable employment environment
The benefits to us	We seek a fair and reasonable return on investment over the long term.

Following an assessment of our values as shown above we have articulated the following mission statement which accurately reflects our broad commercial goals.

Wellbuilt Office Furniture

OUR MISSION STATEMENT

Our corporate mission is to provide people working from small office/home offices in San Diego and surrounding districts with the most efficient and comfortable office work equipment possible.

We further wish to create a secure stable employment environment in which our employees are fairly compensated for reliability, the manufacture of quality products and the provision of excellent customer service.

We seek fair and reasonable return on investment to keep the company financially healthy over the long term while taking our place as responsible employers and good corporate citizens.

2.3 Target markets
(a) Consumer target markets

Consumer target market characteristics	
Product: Work station modules	**Target market:** Small office/home office
Geographics	
Location	San Diego and surrounding districts
Area size	50 square miles
Population	1,223,400
Population density	High
Climate zone	Temperate
Demographics	
Age range	25-55 (Late Baby Boomers/Gen X & Y)
Gender split	60/40 Female/male
Income group	Medium to high
Family composition	Average 4 persons per household
Household type & size	Free standing units
Occupation	Professional
Education	College graduates
Psychographics	
Personality type	High achievers
Behavior characteristics	Strong work ethic, early adopters
Life style	Often combine work with raising families
Rate of use	Daily
Repetition of need	Constant
Benefits sought	Comfort, efficiency, flexibility
Loyalty characteristics	Strong loyalty when needs met
Behavioral	
Needs to be fulfilled	Career and business success
Knowledge level	High
Information sources	Internet
Attitudes	Self-starters
Use or response to a product	Expects and demands the highest quality

2.3 Target markets (cont.)
(b) Business Target Markets

Business target markets characteristics	
Product: Work station modules	Target market: Small office/home office
Business type (manufacturer, retail, wholesale, professional, service)	Professional & service
Industry	Various
Size of business	Micro to small
Financial strength	Sound
Number of employees	1 to 20
Location	San Diego and surrounding district
Employment type	Self employed
Turnover	$100,000 to $500,000 pa
Special considerations	Time poor

KEY POINTS: Based on the target market intelligence assembled we have defined the target markets as being: "Small office/ home office business people who are early adopters of business technology and who are prepared to pay a premium price for the most efficient home office/small office furniture available". Until the product concept had been tested in the market the company will to continue to concentrate sales and distribution in San Diego and surrounding districts before rolling out into other markets when initial progress is consolidated.

2.4 Keys to success

The marketing plan will address all seven keys to success as identified below.

Keys to success	
Product: SoHo Modular work stations	
Keys to success	Comments
Meaningful competitive edge	The modular system is unique and meaningful
Ability to charge a premium price	High technical design with quality materials and workmanship will justify premium price
An effective promotional program	We are confident that our carefully selected promotional program will be effective.
Saturation distribution	We have identified the retailers whose support is critical to our success.
Retail trade support	We have built in an attractive retail margin and a comprehensive retail support program
Interactive e-commerce website	Initially we will promote the e-commerce feature of the site in areas in which we do not have retail distribution
Outstanding customer service	We have plans in place to provide both retail stockists and end users with exceptional customer service.

2.5 Critical Issues

We regard the following critical issues as keys to the success of the plan:

Critical issues	
Product: SoHo Modular work stations	
Critical Issues	Comments
1. The home offices/small offices growth trend is continuing and sustainable	Big business downsizing will maintain the trend to out-sourcing
2. We do not meet any head-to-head competition in the first five years (including imports).	Major competitors do not seem to have yet recognized or focused on the small office/home office trend.
3. The retail trade supports stocking our product	We have a multi-tiered strategy to gain retail trade support. Initial indications are positive.
4. End users accept the modular concept	Preliminary marketing research indicates strong support for the concept.
Other comments: It is essential that we remain focused and do not fall into the trap of spreading our resources too thinly over too many budget items.	

PART 3 MARKETING & SALES OBJECTIVES
3.1 Marketing objectives

Marketing objectives		
Product: Work station modules.		
Market segment: Small offices/home offices		
Marketing Objective	Time frame	How measured
10% share of office furniture purchases in small office and home office market segments	End year 1.	Retail trade data
50% share of office furniture purchases in small office and home office market segments	End year 3.	Retail trade data
Establish awareness of and consumer demand for SoHo brand name	Progressively over the next three years	Telephone surveys among small office/home office proprietors
Expand distribution into Los Angeles	Year 4	Achievement of set revenue and profit goals
Expand distribution into San Francisco	Year 5	As above

KEY POINTS:
After careful analysis summarized in the table above we have defined our marketing objectives as follows:

1. Our immediate goal is to develop a new product segment aimed at Small Office/Home Office (SOHO) business people with the development and release of the best quality, most functional space efficient modular workstation furniture. Specifically we aim to achieve a 10% share of segment by the end of the first year growing to a 50% share by the end of the third year. This will be achieved by persuading small office/home office operators to replace conventional office desks with more efficient SoHo work station modules.

2. At the same time we intend to progressively establish awareness of our brand name among potential users in the first three years

3. We aim to expand distribution of our product into Los Angeles in year 4 and into San Francisco in year 5.

4. Longer-term we intend to develop profitable export markets.

3.2 Sales objectives

Sales Objectives								
Product (or product group): Office furniture								
	Current Year		Year 1 of plan		Year 2 Forecast		Year 3 Forecast	
Existing Products	# of units	$000's	# of units	$000's	# of units	$000's	# of units	$000's
Desks	1,000	700	1,000	700	900	630	800	560
Returns	500	200	500	200	430	180	380	160
Screens	200	100	200	100	180	90	170	85
Total existing products	1,700	1,000	1,700	1,000	1,510	900	1,350	805
New Products (Work stations)	0	0	500	300	1,000	600	1,825	1095
TOTAL ALL PRODUCTS	1,700	1,000	2,200	1,300	2,510	1,500	3,175	1,900

KEY POINTS:

1. Wellbuilt Office Furniture's turnover projections by product show attrition in turnover at a rate of around 10 per cent per annum in respect of desks and returns. Screens sales should diminish at about the same rate.
2. Falling desk and returns turnover will be more than offset by the introduction and growth of workstation modules.
3. The sales objectives we have set are based on our estimates of market size by product segment and are practical in terms of production capacity and working capital finance.
4. The plan shows total sales revenue growing at an annual compound rate of 12% from Year 1 of the plan which we believe is practical and sustainable.

PART 4 MARKETING STRATEGIES
4.1.1 Product development

Product development checklist	
Criteria checklist	Responses
What is the product concept?	High tech/high quality work stations
What are its features?	Compact integration of computers and peripherals
What are its benefits?	Improved functionality and efficiency
What is the proposed target market	Small offices and home offices
Will this product replace an existing product or create a new product segment?	Replaces conventional desks and other office furniture
Can it be produced with our existing facilities?	Yes with minor modifications
What pricing strategy is envisaged?	Premium price to fit premium quality strategy
How will it be branded?	Under the 'Soho" brand
How will it be distributed?	Via office supply chains and general furniture retailers
How will it be packaged?	In ready to assemble flat pack kits
How will it be communicated to the target market?	Media advertising, trade shows, in-store displays retailers cooperative ads and catalogues
Which products will it compete against?	Conventional office desks and tables
What market research is proposed?	Focus groups among target market
What is the market research budget	$10,000
What is the product development budget?	$30,000
What is the proposed marketing budget?	$480,000
What are the perceived risks?	Time it takes and cost of getting the message across to a critical mass of customers
What is the proposed launch date?	February 2018

KEY POINTS:

Encouraged by positive market research results and after working through the points covered in the above product development checklist, we are committed to base our future on developing high end premium quality workstations for small offices/home offices that meet the following criteria:

1. Space and energy efficient hi tech/high quality that allows compact integration of computers and peripherals with built-in facilities for cable management Internet sockets and power supplies. They will also include built-in fluorescent light fittings and adjustable arms for computer screens.
2. They will have sit/stand capability. The units will be in module form for future expansion flexibility. A unique locking device will be developed to enable ease of assembly without the need for special tools. The modules will be produced in a range of high end scratch resistant finishes and colors.

The product development schedule is as follows:

Product development schedule		
Product development stage	Target completion date	Responsibility
Production of prototype or sample	Mid 2017	Dennis/Mark
Marketing & trade research	September 2017	Mark
Finalize packaging design	October 2017	Dennis
Commence commercial production	January 2018	Mark
Trade launch date	February 2018	Mark
Commence distribution	March 2018	Mark
Consumer launch date	April 2018	Mark
Post launch evaluation	June 2018	Mark/Dennis

4.1.2 Product proposition

Product proposition development		
Product: SoHo work station modules		
Product proposition options	Proposition Expression	Scale of appeal Rating 1-10
Efficiency and functionality	Higher productivity in less work space	10
Sit or stand functionality	Adjustable desk top provides healthy circulation and movement options	8
Product design	Modular office furniture functionality for computerized offices	7
Product quality	Timber not chipboard	5
Preferred primary product proposition expression: "SoHo work stations deliver more productivity in less work space".		

KEY POINTS:
Recognizing that floor space in small offices is invariably at a premium, the product proposition developed for our workstation modules is:
 "SoHo work stations deliver more productivity in less work space".
Product features we will promote are:
- Quality materials
- Functionality
- Unique features
- Ease of assembly
- Modular for future expansion
- Ergonomic design
- Sit or stand functionality
- Space efficient

4.1.3 Product Positioning

Product positioning statement development		
Product: ScHo work station modules		
Positioning options checklist	Positioning statement	Scale of uniqueness rating 1 to 10
User group	For the small Office/Home Office".	10
Product quality and functionality	The ultimate in high tech quality and functionality	10
Price and quality	At the premium end of the price scale	10
Price & service	Not applicable in this example	0
Usage occasions	Not applicable in this example	0
Store environment and product range	Not applicable in this example	0
Preferred positioning statement: "The ultimate in modular high tech/functional work stations for state-of-the-art Small Offices/Home Offices".		

KEY POINT: Following development of a positioning map in which price/quality and office size were set as variables we have concluded that the prime opportunity for Wellbuilt is in the premium quality/price small office/home office sector of the market. This position is not 'occupied' by any of the major office furniture manufacturers at present.

4.1.4 Branding

Brand selection checklist
Product: SoHo work station modules
Q. Is our corporate brand name widely recognized in the market in which we compete? ☒ Yes ☑ No
Q. If 'yes' would the addition of a description of the product or service category to the corporate name add to business identity and positioning? ☐ Yes ☐ No. Not applicable in this instance.
Q. Would the introduction of an original brand name offer marketing advantages? ☑ **Yes** ☒ **No**
Q. If 'yes' what are they? Describes and positions the product concept
Q. What branding strategy do our main competitors use? ☑ Corporate ☒ Original
Q. Are competitors' branding strategies more effective than ours? ☐ Yes ☑ No (At least not at present).
Q. Do we have access to potential brand names that could be developed? ☑ Yes ☒ No
Q. Are we prepared to invest resources required in the development of an original brand? ☑ Yes ☒ No
Q. Is there potential in the market for the introduction of a 'price' brand in addition to our established brand? ☐ Yes ☑ No At least not in the foreseeable future
Summary: We intend to market our product under the brand name 'SoHo' because it meets the criteria we are looking for.

CONCLUSIONS:

1. Since we have never made a conscious effort to develop the company name as a brand name widely recognized by end users there is little or no recognition or awareness of the name *Wellbuilt Office* Furniture among end users or the broader community.

2. We therefore see an opportunity to start with a clean slate using a new brand name that positions the new product concept and which we can develop over time to build a consumer franchise in the market segments we intend to target.

3. This sector is commonly referred to as the SOHO (Small Office/Home Office) sector. A search of the trades marks register has revealed that the trademark "SOHO" is available for registration in the appropriate product category and we intend to seize this opportunity.

4. We therefore intend to market our new product range as SoHo Modular Work Stations.

5. Upon registration of the trademark we intend to develop a logo, which will graphically communicate the product concept.

6. We are also considering an innovation in furniture branding. Unlike other consumer durable product categories (such as electrical appliances and computer systems, etc.) furniture products are rarely identified by brand name. Even if consumers are aware of the brand name of the product they are buying at the time of purchase the brand name is often quickly forgotten after purchase in the absence of a reminder.

7. We will therefore trial a discrete stylish brass plate stamped with the brand name, web address and the free call number we have taken out for product service and enquiries. These plates will be fixed to each module in a non-obtrusive but visible position. We anticipate that this device will aid brand awareness and lead to referrals and repeat purchasing.

4.1.5 Brand & corporate image

Brand (or) corporate image checklist
Q. What do we know about our current brand (or corporate) image among customers, prospects, suppliers and others in contact with the company?
A. Our company name is not established with the general public. We are therefore intending to establish a more descriptive and distinctive name for the proposed new product concept
Q. What do we want the brand image to be?
A. Technologically advanced, premium quality, state-of-the-art.
Q. If our brand was a person, what images attributes would we want to convey?
A. Solid, reliable, young, dynamic, dependable, clever, entrepreneurial, innovative, early adopter.
Q. How does our image compare with our nearest competitors?
A. As yet there are no significant competitors in the product segment we intend to enter
Q. How well does our current visual corporate identity contribute towards the desired brand image?
A. We will develop a new visual corporate identity in keeping with the desired brand image
Q. What steps can we take to strengthen the desired brand image among our customers, prospects, employees, suppliers and others?
A. We will portray the desired attributes in our website, advertising, promotions, packaging, pricing and social media and in all other corporate communications.

We understand that brand image cannot be established overnight but we intend to develop a brand image for *SoHo* over time that reflects the following brand image attributes:

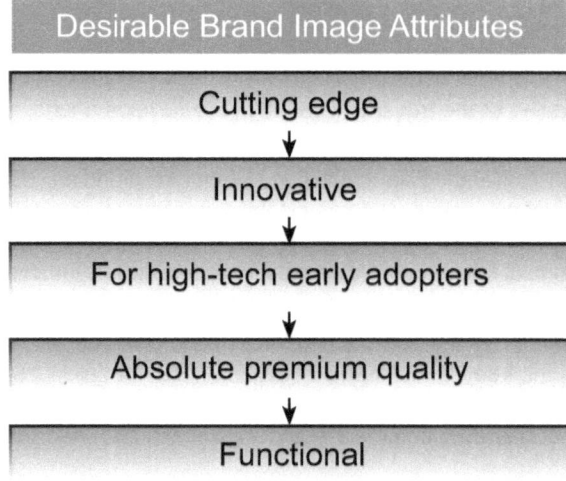

4.1.6 Packaging

Packaging Checklist		
Criteria	Functionality	Graphics
What are the pros and cons of our packaging materials?	Our proposed packaging will be in well-designed 'flat packs' for economy in storage and transportation.	Eye catching graphics will illustrate the product concept, highlight the brand name and help to merchandise the product at the retail level.
What are the pros and cons of our main competitors packaging materials?	Not direct competitors at this stage	Not yet applicable.
What can we do to improve our packaging's functionality and design graphics	We will constantly monitor improvement opportunities and seek the advice of packaging suppliers.	We will study Ikeas approach to flat pack packaging and graphics as they are the leaders in the category.

KEY POINTS:

Mindful of the need to distribute products in ready to assemble form we have engaged the services of a packaging design consultant to meet the following criteria:

1. Adequate outer and inner protection of all component parts. In "flat-packs" for compact storage, transportation and merchandising.

2. Eye catching graphics in which the brand name will be prominent, will illustrate the concept and merchandise the product when it is shelved and displayed in the forward display area of retail stores. The graphics will portray our product proposition and positioning with reference to ease of assembly. Assembly instructions will be included in an easy to follow step-by-step format.

4.2 Price
4.2.1 Price strategies

Competitive pricing analysis					
Product	List price $	End user price $	Retail Mark up	Retail Markup %	Retail Gross Margin %
Our product	$600 per module	$900 per module	$300	50%	33%
Competitor 1 Bettabilt	$500	$700	$200	40%	29%
Competitor 2 Stylecraft	$450	$650	$200	44%	31%
Competitor 3 Colonial	$400	$600	$200	50%	33%

There are no direct competitors in this product segment which is a major reason for placing our faith in entering this market niche.

Proposed Pricing strategies			
The pricing strategies we intend to adopt are:			
☐ Cost plus	☐ Market skimming	☐ Market penetration	☐ Loss Leader
☑ Premium pricing	☐ Parity pricing	☐ Commodity pricing	☐ Captive pricing
The rationale for adopting these options is: We have a quality product with little or no direct competition. Premium pricing will allow us to fund marketing and trade support. Our research indicated potential users are prepared to pay around $900 per module given the benefits they provide.			

KEY POINTS:

As this is a unique product with no direct competition in the market and product segments we have targeted from either local manufacturers or imports, we are confident we can adopt a price premium strategy. This policy will provide:
1. Funds for marketing support;
2. Better than average margins for retailers
3. Consistency with the brand image and positioning
4. The ability to use quality materials and workmanship.
5. An allowance for continuing R&D and investment in marketing.

Our RRP will be set at around $900 per module. This will provide a retail mark-up of 50% (or 33% gross margin) on a list price of $600 per module. Initial concept research conducted confirmed that customers will be prepared to pay up to $1,000 for the benefits our products will deliver.

4.2.2 Price tactics

Proposed price tactics			
The pricing tactics we intend to adopt are:			
☑ Short term discounts	☑ Quantity discounts	☑ Promotional allowances	
☑ Special payment or credit terms	☐ Consignment terms	☐ Refund policy	☐ Bundling

KEY POINTS: The rationale for adopting these options is:

1. A 5% discount on quantities of 25 units or more will encourage maintenance of adequate stock levels
2. A further 5% discount will be paid for on floor displays and temporary price reductions tied in with retailers' catalogue sales.
3. We are also prepared to provide credit terms of 30 days from invoice.

These tactics will be monitored on an ongoing basis and adjusted as deemed appropriate.

4.3 Place
4.3.1 Business location

Business location analysis	
To what extent does the site affect your business	Not to any major extent as the site is not a retail outlet - but we do intend to develop an upscale showroom in due course.
What is the rate of passing traffic?	Extensive
Is the site rental high, low or average?	We own the site.
Is passing traffic commensurate with rent?	Not applicable
Is the building in keeping with your desired image?	Not at present but we intend to upgrade the showroom.
What is the extent of direct competition?	None
Are there complementary businesses in your area?	No.
Is customer parking adequate?	Yes.
Is there enough space for your operations?	Yes for the foreseeable future.
Are there signage opportunities to attract customers?	Yes.
Is the site close to residential or commercial zones from which your customer base is drawn?	Yes
Is the location developing, reaching maturity or in decline?	Reaching maturity
Should we consider moving to a better location?	Not in the foreseeable future.

KEY POINTS:
1. As Wellbuilt Furniture is not a retail business our location is not a primary concern.
2. We do however intend to make better use of the available space we have in the front office area to develop a showroom where we can display and demonstrate the product range to retailer buyers and potential end users.
3. We do not intend to make the showroom a retail outlet with sales direct to the public so any orders received at the showroom will be referred to retailers to maintain retail trade relations.
4. We believe that an outdoor illuminated sign on the showroom frontage will help develop product and brand awareness, as the volume of passing traffic is extensive.

4.3.2 Distribution channels

		Distribution channels checklist		
Product	Target market	Existing distribution channels	Efficiency ranking 1 to 10	Proposed changes (if any)
Free standing executive desks (existing products)	Small to medium corporate customers	Direct to specialized office furniture retailers	6	We may phase out of this market if the launch of our proposed new work station module product line is successful
Work station modules (proposed new product range)	Small offices/Home offices	Direct to office furniture retailers, domestic furniture retailers, office supply chains and (later) Internet ecommerce marketing	Not yet tested	To be assessed after initial launch stage

KEY POINTS:

Firstly we intend to protect and maintain distribution of our existing products through our established network of office furniture retailers in San Diego and surrounding districts. We will also introduce our new SoHo range to them to encourage sales to medium and large corporate customers.

We are aware however that this will be inadequate to meet our newly defined corporate goals and we therefore intend to take the following steps to extend distribution to meet the set targets.

1. We will present the range to selected general furniture retail outlets with particular emphasis on home office furniture stockists.
2. We will aggressively seek distribution of our products through office supply chains (such as OfficeWorks) that retail office furniture along with stationery, computer supplies etc. and which often merchandise floor displays of office furniture for small and home office customers. These retailers feature office furniture in product catalogs and flyers which we will participate in and contribute to.
3. We will develop a website designed to market our products nationally or even internationally. The website will serve as both an advertising medium and as an ecommerce channel.
4. When the new range is sufficiently established in our home base, we will investigate the feasibility of appointing wholesalers, distributors and agents with a view to expanding distribution of the product range to other selected domestic market regions.

4.3.3 Distribution channel partners business maximization

Distribution channel partners maximization checklist		
Product	Distribution Channel	Proposed Development Strategies
Work station modules	Office supply chains	Build floor displays of assembled modules. Merchandise with quality point-of-sale materials
Work station modules	Domestic furniture retailers	As above
Work station modules	Office furniture retailers	Set up regular meetings for sales progress reviews. Invite key contacts to factory/showroom sales events.
Tables, seating, storage etc.	All existing channels	Maintain all current programs to sustain distribution of existing products as long as possible.

KEY POINTS:

Channel partners business maximization strategies we intend to pursue will include:

1. Allocation of financial and labor resources to build floor displays of assembled work station modules to allow potential end users to view assembled modules.
2. Supply distribution channel partners with well-designed premium quality point-of-sale and merchandising materials.

4.3.4 Supply chain management

Supply chain checklist		
Supply chain stage	Existing efficiency rating (Scale 1 to 10)	Proposed changes to shorten the chain
Raw materials to factory	6	Keep tighter inventory control on raw materials stock levels at factory and place orders at predetermined trigger points
Factory to distribution channels	5	Maintain closer checks of finished product stock levels at distributors and agents and replenish stock levels before stock outs
Distribution channels to retailers	6	Keep closer controls on stock levels at retail level and ensure distributors and agents can supply stock at short notice
Factory to retailers	7	Closely monitor stock levels at retailers and ensure factory can supply direct orders within two working days. Implement 'just in time' inventory management system.

KEY POINTS:

We are acutely aware that 'out-of-stocks' and unavailability of product to meet consumer demand is frustrating to manufacturers, retailers and end-consumers alike. We therefore intend to minimize impediments to sales through implementing the following procedures:

1. We will keep close checks on raw material stock levels in the factory and place orders at set trigger points.
2. We will monitor finished product stock levels in our factory warehouse and at distributors and agents to replenish stocks before "out-of-stocks" occur.
3. We will closely monitor stock levels at retailers to ensure stocks are replenished at short notice.
4. We are confident these measures will give us a clear competitive advantage particularly against imported products where long lead times apply.

4.4 Promotion
4.4.1 Sales management

We intend to appoint a full time sales representative to our team who will share sales calls with Mark.

Using these resources we have developed a number of programs, as outlined below, to ensure sales targets are achieved.

Sales management functions checklist		
Function	Efficiency rating (Scale of 1 to 10)	Proposed action
Sales reps coverage of potential market	6	We intend to increase sales representative coverage from 60% of available retail outlets to 80% with the addition of one more salesman to service retailers outside the main metropolitan area
Call cycle frequency	7	We will grade retailers by potential sales volume and structure sales calls accordingly. "A" grade stores will receive fortnightly calls. "B" grade stores will receive monthly calls and "C" grade stores will be allocated bimonthly calls.
Quality of sales reps calls	7	We will provide sales persons with up to date computer generated customer records so that they can present sales status to retail buyers with suggested improvement opportunities
Sales territory allocation efficiency	6	We will conduct regular reviews to ensure minimum sales territory overlaps.
Quality of service to retail trade	7	We will provide sales persons with quality materials to allow them to professionally present industry trends and new product updates.
Sales training	4	We have neglected this area of our operations and intend to appoint external sales trainers to conduct half yearly training workshops on different aspects of the sales function.

4.4.2 Sales development
a) Existing customers
We are committed to pursue each of the five basic sales development strategies in our marketing programs. These are:

Retain existing customers
Raise the average sales value
Encourage repeat purchasing
Reinstate lapsed users
Expand the customer base

Sales development techniques - existing customers	
Sales technique	Proposed actions
Up selling	Offer work station customers a 10% cash back offer to upgrade to new product releases
Cross selling	Offer work station purchasers a 10% cash back offer on office chairs
Volume discounts	Offer retailers a 15% discount for two or more work station modules with a 10% discount passed on to consumers.
Reward programs	Offer customers a free computer monitor arm on three consecutive purchases in a two year period.
Bundling	Offer work station customers a 5% discount on the purchase of a small side table bundled with a work station
Incremental selling	Offer work station customers a 20% cashback with an additional purchase of a work station screen
NOTE: Offers to existing customers will be communicated via our proposed database email marketing program	

4.4.2 Sales development (cont.)
b) New customers

We will diligently pursue all means at our disposal to continuously attract new customers through utilization of the five techniques described below.

Sales development techniques - new customers	
Sales technique	Proposed actions
Personal recommendation	We will offer existing customers a 10% discount on their next purchase when they 'refer a friend' that results in a work station purchase.
Cold canvassing	We will develop a cold canvassing program at retail level calling on potential stockists via personal selling, telesales and email marketing.
Networking	We will join the Small Business Association in our area with a view to delivering presentations and networking among other small business owner operators.
Advertising	We will advertise in selected newspapers and small business magazines.
Internet marketing	We will develop a first class interactive website and invest in search engine advertising.

4.4.3 Customer service

We intend to gain a competitive edge through providing our retail customers and end users with high standards of customer service. We regard our customers as ongoing – not once only purchasers. Our servicing plans are outlined below:

Customer service action checklist		
Customer service functions	Efficiency rating (Scale 1 to 10)	Proposed actions
Customer focus	5	We intend to consult retail stockists in the development of the new range. We will assist them with merchandising and advertising. We will also conduct market research among potential end users
Product knowledge	6	We will communicate our products advantages over the competition to retail stockists and end users. We will supply buyers with regular updates on market segment trends.
Customer communications	7	We will maintain close liaison with retail stockists to ensure they are carrying adequate but not excessive stocks. We will make sure we maintain a customer contact schedule that suits their individual needs. We will maintain a dedicated help section in our website and have a free call consumer advice facility.
Customer relations	7	We will honor our commitments to our trade customers to the letter and assist them wherever possible to improve their turnover in the product category. We will also provide end users with 12 month warranties on workmanship and parts.

4.5 Advertising
4.5.1 Advertising objectives
After careful consideration we have set our advertising objectives as follows:

Advertising objectives	
Advertising Objective	How measured
PRIMARY Generate sales enquiries and convert enquiries to sales at the six principal retail stockists.	Sales recorded by each of the six principal stockists within two months of each advertising cycle.
SECONDARY 1 Gain prominent display space support from retail stockists by directing store traffic to them from our advertising and cooperative trade advertising.	We will maintain a register of retail display floor space allocated by each of the retailers listed in print advertisements, before, during and after advertising scheduling.
SECONDARY 2 Create interest and enquiries from retailers not currently stocking our products	We will create and maintain a database system that will record all stages of sales development from initial contact to customer conversion.

4.5.2 Advertising responsibilities allocation
Sales and Marketing Manager Mark Miller will be responsible for all aspects of company advertising.

As our advertising budget is deemed too small to warrant the appointment of an advertising agency we will use the creative services of the media with whom advertising is placed. We will also call upon the services of a marketing consultant in an advisory capacity and engage freelance specialists as required.

Advertising responsibilites allocation		
Advertising function	Scheduled completion date	Person responsible
Advertising budget allocation	Mid 2017	Mark/Dennis
Setting the advertising brief	September 2017	Mark
Media selection	September 2017	Mark
Allocation of creative resources and development of creative material	October 2017	Mark
Advertising material approval	January 2018	Mark
Media placement	April 2018	Mark

4.5.3 Advertising budget setting

After consideration of the key factors shown below we have determined that we will initially commit 7% of budgeted gross revenue to advertising (including cooperative advertising). If budgeted revenue remains on track as the year progresses, we will commit up to 10% of gross revenue to advertising. A breakdown of the advertising spend is detailed in the consolidated marketing budget.

Advertising budget setting	
Considerations	Comments
Fixed % of budgeted revenue	Based on gross revenue of $1.3M, (existing and new products) we have resolved that we are prepared to spend up to 37% of gross revenue on marketing in year 1 to establish the new product range. Within this we will invest around 7% of gross revenue on advertising. This equates to an advertising budget of $91,000
Acceptable investment level	We consider that an initial advertising budget of $91,000 is an acceptable investment in advertising in Year 1. We have allocated a reserve of $39,000 in the overall marketing budget, which will be added to the advertising budget if budgeted revenue remains on track or if it is exceeded. This would create a maximum advertising budget of 10% of gross sales.
Past spend levels	We have not advertised to any extent in the past.
Cost estimate on a line by line basis of media and production costs	We have estimated that the budget allocated is adequate to fund the scale of advertising we require to achieve the set objectives.
Competitors' spend levels	We do not yet have any direct competitors with whom to compare spend levels.
Advertising budget allocation ($'s)	Up to a maximum of $100,000 in year 1 (including contingency).

4.5.4 The creative brief

Following a careful strategic review we have summarized the creative brief below consistent with all other elements of the marketing plan.

The creative brief	
Product or service:	SoHo workstation modules
Overall marketing objective:	Create and dominate a new product segment in our home market.
Primary advertising objective:	Create consumer awareness, generate sales enquiries and convert enquiries to sales at the six designated principal retail stockists
Secondary advertising objective:	Gain prominent display space and sales support from stockists by directing sales traffic to them from our advertising
Target market:	Small office/home office decision makers who are early adopters of new high-end technology.
Product proposition:	"SoHo work stations deliver higher productivity in less floor space".
Product positioning:	Cutting edge work stations for the small office/home office
Desired brand image:	Technologically advanced, premium quality, flexible in use
Desired net impression:	The ultimate in small office/home office furniture for advanced users of computer technology
Advertising budget:	The total ad budget is up to a maximum of $100,000 for Year 1

4.5.5 Media selection

In reviewing the available media options we have concluded that highly targeted print media would be ideal to illustrate the modular product concept including the unique product feature we have developed.

We have decided to allocate a significant part of our marketing budget on participation in retailers' cooperative advertising and catalogs in the first year. In doing this we believe it will serve the purpose of directing the target audience to the point-of-purchase while helping to gain support from participating stockists in the allocation of free or low cost in-store display space. In addition we will:

1. Place advertisements in newspaper and magazine features targeted at small office/home office managers.
2. Produce dedicated product brochures and flyers for distribution at point-of-sale.
3. Place a small display advertisement in the Yellow Pages.
4. Produce high quality sales presenters as tools for the "sell-in" of the new product range.
5. Erect on-site signage at our premises to advertise the new product range to passing traffic.
6. We have also made an allocation for social media advertising as this medium is appropriate for our 'tech savvy' target market.

Media selection checklist		
Product: SoHo modular work stations		
☑ Cost effective reach of target market	☑ Retention of ads for future reference	☑ Ability to offer discount or other offer coupons
☑ Show the product	☑ List product stockists	☑ High impact
☒ Color	☒ Sound (audio)	☒ Movement (video)
☑ Short lead times	☑ Low production costs	☑ List product benefits
☑ List product specifications	☑ Response rate measurement	☑ Repetition
Preferred media option/s ☒TV ☒ Radio ☑ Newspapers ☑ Magazines ☒ Outdoor ☒ Cinema ☑ Cooperative trade advertising ☑Social media advertising ☒ Third party websites ☒ Search engine advertising ☑ *Yellow pages and* other directories ☒ Other (Specify)		
Geographical markets we need to reach: San Diego and surrounding districts		
Budget allocated: Up to a maximum of $100,000 in Year 1		
Conclusions: Print media meets our criteria more efficiently than electronic media. We envisage a mix of ads in local newspapers supplemented with participation in cooperative retailers advertising and catalogs. We will experiment with social media advertising as this medium is appropriate to reach our tech savvy millennials target market.		

4.5.6 Advertising research

As our advertising budget is comparatively small the use of external research resources is not initially warranted. Instead we will implement a series of effective but low cost measures as shown below.

Advertising research	
Method	Comments
Measure store traffic before and after advertising	We will actively seek and monitor retailers feedback
Discount and cashback coupons	We will experiment with cashback offers in selected print media to gauge response rates
Dedicated telephone hotline number	We will have a dedicated hotline phone number to measure the Yellow Pages advertising response rate
Customer surveys	We will consider implementing a customer survey in the second year which will include questions relating to how customers became aware of our products
Seek customers feedback	We will conduct a telephone survey to measure advertising awareness upon receipt of customers' warranty cards.
Website 'hits'	We will use Google Analytics to measure website 'hit's before during and after advertising scheduling.

4.6 Sales promotion

Mindful of the need to get the new product range off to a successful start we have allocated funds to finance the following promotional activities:

1. Promotional DVD: We will produce a promotional DVD to demonstrate the functionality of the range and ease of assembly to show at trade shows and exhibitions as well as on a rotating basis in selected retail outlets.
2. Cash incentives and allowances: We will provide cash incentives for product listings and floor displays on a managed rolling basis. This will be overlaid with allowances for periodic temporary price reductions or cash backs tied in with participation in dealers' catalogues and promotions
3. Promotional merchandise: We intend to produce a supply of promotional merchandise such as branded caps, T-shirts, diaries and calendars for distribution to dealers at the trade launch function and the office furniture exhibition.

Sales promotion planning schedule

Product: SoHo work modular stations

Objective	Promotion type	Timing & duration	Budget $'s	Coordin-ator
Create retail trade awareness & interest	Hold a product launch function for retailers to sell the new range	End 2016	10,000	Mark
Gain distribution and floor displays in retail stockists	Provide cash incentives and allowances for product listings and floor displays on a selective basis.	Two week promotions each quarter in the first year	30,000	Mark
Maintain trade and consumer interest and sales impetus	Periodic price reductions tied in with retailers advertising and promotions.	Two week promotions tied in with retail promotions and floor displays	20,000	Mark
Demonstrate the functionality and ease of assembly of the new product line to the trade and end users.	Produce a promotional DVD for use at trade shows and displays at selected retail stockists.	On a selective rotating basis	10,000	Mark
Establish and maintain awareness of the brand and product range	Produce a supply of promotional merchandise such as branded caps, T-Shirts, diaries and calendars.	In the initial four week product launch period	5,000	Mark

4.7 Trade shows and exhibitions

We have allocated funds for a stand at the *FURNITEX* office furniture exhibition to present the new range to the retail trade and potential end users among the public. The stand will be manned by Mark and the new sales representative. We will display assembled SoHo work station modules, demonstrate the product's features and screen the proposed promotional DVD.

Trade shows and exhibitions activity schedule		
Product	SoHo work station modules	
Trade show name	FURNITEX office furniture exhibition	
Target market	Retail trade buyers and Small office/home office workers	
Objective	Present the new range to the retail trade and potential end users	
Proposed activities	We will reserve a small stand to display assembled SoHo work station modules, demonstrate the product's features and screen the proposed promotional DVD. We will also use the event to write orders and provide trade hospitality.	
Timing & duration	Budget $'s	Coordinator
March 10 -17, 2019	15,000	Mark

4.8 Online marketing and ecommerce
4.8.1 Website functionality
A quality highly functional website is a key part of our marketing strategy as our target market is very internet savvy. Website functions, contents, actions and maintenance checklists are summarized in the checklist below.

Website functionality requirements	
Product: SoHo modular work stations	
What functions do we require from our website?	☑ Showcase our products ☑ Generate sales enquiries via contact links ☑ Create databases for sales leads ☑ Conduct ecommerce transactions via the Internet ☑ Content management system ☑ Database email marketing facility ☐ Other
Contents checklist	☑ Product range catalogue ☑ Competitive advantages list ☑ Company history, mission statement and executives profiles ☑ email contact facility ☑ Shopping cart facility ☑ Credit card transaction facilities
Content marketing	Continually create and post items of interest such as: ☑ Blogs, ☑ eBooks, ☑ Press releases and other text based items of interest to our target market as well as ☑ Videos and podcasts
Action checklist	☑ Determine and assemble content ☑ Register web address ☑ Engage website designer ☑ Appoint internet service provider ☑ Appoint web server ☑ Arrange merchant (credit card transaction) facilities ☑ Exchange links with complementary sites
Maintenance checklist	☑ Continually improve and update web graphics and content ☑ Continually improve products/ services featured on the site ☑ Continue to seek new links with complementary sites ☑ Continue to place strategic advertising on search engines/analyze results/refine markets/budgets and key words ☑ Measure website traffic data with Google Analytics and make adjustments based on the data reported.

4.8.2 Website promotion strategies

We are conscious that websites need to be constantly updated and promoted. To this end we will implement a program comprised of website promotion, Search Engine Optimization (SEO) and Search Engine Advertising (SEA).

Web site promotion strategies	
Product: SoHo modular work stations	
Website promotion checklist	☑ Include URL in all new stationery ☑ Include URL in all sales materials ☑ Include URL in all email signatures ☑ Include URL in all print and advertising materials
Search engine optimization (SEO)	☑ Submit the site to all major search engines including Google, Yahoo, Bing and AltaVista. ☑ Appoint a SEO specialist to ensure the site is search engine friendly ☑ Include ample high quality content in the site
Search engine advertising	☑ Conduct trials with different keywords in Google's 'AdWords' ☑ Select target markets (countries/regions/cities/languages). ☑ Research and write ad text and select keywords ☑ Set pricing – cost per click and budget per period ☑ Monitor ongoing results from online performance reports and modify strategy accordingly.
Comments: We will constantly monitor Google Analytics to measure and analyze the source of our website traffic in order to maximize the effectiveness of the site.	

4.8.3 Social media marketing

We have become increasingly aware of the growth of importance of businesses creating a conduit with consumers and the retail trade via social media platforms. We understand the importance of creating and maintaining a presence in the main platforms especially given that our customer base is very internet savvy and are even more likely to follow business social media sites than the average person.

We also wish to maintain an effective communications program with our customers to ensure that our products meet our customer's needs and to obtain value customer feedback so that our product development program delivers what users want as opposed to what we can make.

Social media marketing programs		
Product: SoHo work station modules		
Platform	Target market	Objectives
Facebook	Small office/home office customers and prospects	1. Interact with users of our products and obtain feedback on their likes and dislikes of their experience with our work station modules. 2. Encourage users to recommend our products to their peers and associates.
Twitter	As above	As above,
LinkedIn	Office furniture retailers	1. Convey positive updates in relation to the progress of the launch program. 2. Persuade non-stockists to stock our products in their stores. 3. Use the site to communicate trade nights and presentations.
YouTube	Small office/home office customers and prospects	Demonstrate SoHo work station modules features and ease of assembly. Embed the video in a prominent place in our website.
Blog platforms	Generations Y & Z	We will maintain a presence on popular blog platforms such as WordPress and BlogSpot.
Comments: We will also consider a presence in Google+ when the above platforms are bedded down and functioning efficiently.		

4.9 Merchandising

We understand the need to ensure our products are prominently displayed on retail floors while acknowledging the competition that exists for available floor a space.

Initially we are prepared to consider consignment stock supply for floor displays if this enables us to secure initial listings with retailers who we have identified as priority stockists of our products.

Our merchandising program is summarized below:

Merchandising program – Year 1.		
Retail Outlet/Store Type	Proposed Merchandising Activity	Proposed Merchandising Materials
Office supply chains (e.g. Officeworks)	Floor stack displays of flat packs where display space is limited. Supplement with show cards and posters showing assembled product. We will supply the labor to build the displays if required by retailers.	Large strutted show cards. A3 size posters Flyers for distribution at point-of sale to highlight the modular expansion concept, the locking device feature, the sit/stand feature and product dimension details.
Office furniture retailers	Floor displays of assembled products. Supplement displays with quality point of sale materials	Flyers for take home reference
Domestic furniture retailers	As above	As above

4.10 Public Relations and Publicity

Public relations & publicity activity program	
Product: SoHo work station modules	
Program 1 description	Press kit for product launch
Objectives	Gain publicity to create awareness and generate interest in the new range.
Target market	Potential end users and decision makers in the office supply and retail furniture outlets we have targeted.
Proposed media	Specialized office furniture and computer technology magazines.
Format	The kit will include quality photography of the product concept in a work environment situation. The kit will refer to market dynamics which have inspired the product's development, the market gap the range will fill and the unique product features developed for the new product line. Copies of published articles will be sent to potential stockists via a direct mail.
Budget allocated	$5,000
Program 2 description	Trade and media function
Objectives	Gain publicity to create awareness and generate interest in the new range.
Target market	Decision makers in the office supply and retail furniture outlets we have targeted. Specialized office furniture and computer technology magazines journalists
Proposed media	Specialized office furniture and computer technology magazines.
Format	Tied in with the furniture exhibition in which we will participate we will invite key trade customers and trade magazine journalists to an organized launch function at our exhibition stand where they will be able to view assembled samples of the new range. We will provide first class catering, entertainment and door prizes to stimulate interest.
Budget allocated	$16,000

KEY POINTS:
1. As we have produced a new concept in office furniture we believe the story has sufficient news value to be of interest to specialist small business, computer and trade magazines.
2. We therefore intend to produce a press kit complete with high quality digital photography and a professionally written media release that will describe the product concept in detail and show it in a work situation environment.
3. The press kit will be mass circulated to furniture, small business and

computer technology magazines nationally. It will include market dynamics that have led to the development of the new product and detail the unique product features developed for the range.
4. Copies of published articles will be circulated to current and potential retailers with personalized letters.
5. As a trade relations exercise we intend to invite key trade buyers and trade magazine journalists to a launch function at our showroom where they will be able to view assembled samples of the new range. We will provide first class catering, entertainment and door prizes at the function.

4.11 Sponsorship

We will cosponsor the "Small Business of the Year" award at the Furnitex Office Furniture exhibition in which we will participate. This will give us the opportunity to get a 'plug' at the prize presentation ceremony and in the competition entry form. Sponsorship will give us access to the entrants contact details to enable us to run a direct mail campaign to reach this prime target market.

Other low cost sponsorship opportunities will be evaluated on a cost/benefit basis as opportunities arise.

Proposed sponsorship programs	
Product: SoHo work station modules	
Program description	Co-sponsorship of the 'Small Business of the Year' award at the Furnitex Exhibition
Objectives	Contribute to the development of an awareness profile for the new range.
Target market	Potential end users and decision makers in the office supply and retail furniture outlets we have targeted.
Benefits	We will gain the opportunity to address the audience at the prize presentation ceremony. We will have prominent branding in the competition entry form and other associated literature. We will have access to all the entrants contact details to enable us to conduct email-marketing campaigns targeted to this prime target market.
Budget allocated	The cost will be limited to the donation of a SoHo workstation module to the winner of the award.

4.12 Corporate Communications

We will produce a small but selective range of corporate communications materials to assist our sales activities at both trade and consumer levels.

Template 49 - Corporate communications materials program (example)		
Product: SoHo work station modules		
Item	Communications objectives	Target market
Glossy product brochure in hard copy and pdf formats	For use as a sales presenter to assist in gaining retail trade orders	Office furniture retailers
Product flyers for use as a handout at point-of-sale, and trade exhibitions and as a utility mailer.	To provide potential customers with detailed product information including product specifications.	Prospective end users
Video for screening at trade exhibitions, in-store displays and the corporate website.	Demonstrate benefits such as ease of assembly and functionality	Prospective end users and retail trade buyers.

4.13 Direct Marketing and Database Marketing

Mindful of the cost efficiency of direct marketing we will develop and maintain trade and consumer databases that will give us the opportunity to keep in close touch with our customers at retail trade and consumer levels. The consumer data base will be compiled from on-line product registrations supplemented with 'newsletter subscribes' received from the website and other sources.

Direct marketing & database marketing programs checklist		
Product: SoHo work station modules		
Program	Communications objectives	Target market
email marketing	'Up sell' and 'cross sell' Communicate work station modules benefits	Small office and home office purchasers and potential purchasers
Direct mail	Pre-sell the concept to retailers prior to sales reps initial sales call.	Potential retail buyers
Telesales	Promote awareness of the product line and schedule sales call appointments and monitor retail stock levels	Retail buyers and store managers.

PART 5 FINANCIAL STATEMENTS

5.1 Marketing Budget

The marketing budget for Year 1 has been allocated as detailed below: This represents an investment of around one third of total revenue in Year 1 to allow us to successfully launch the new range. We are fully aware that the spend level is high, however we have taken the view that an aggressive launch program is needed to develop and claim market leadership of the new product segment. The ratio of marketing spend to revenue will be gradually scaled back in subsequent years as the income generated by the new range grows to a more sustainable level.

Marketing budget - Year 1

Item	Budget $	Item	Budget $	Item	Budget $
MEDIA ADVERTISING		PRINT		OTHER	
TV & radio	-	Corporate brochures & flyers	20,000	Public relations & publicity	5,000
Newspapers & magazines	35,000	Sales presenters	10,000	Trade functions	16,000
Cooperative trade advertising	40,000	Product catalogues	30,000	Marketing research	10,000
Social media advertising	3,000	Merchandising & display materials	40,000	Showroom upgrade	50,000
Directory advertising	1,000			Packaging materials design	5,000
Media production costs	5,000			Product development	30,000
Ad agency & consultants fees	7,000			Sponsorships	2,000
Other	-			Signage	10,000
SUB TOTAL	91,000	SUB TOTAL	100,000	SUB TOTAL	128,000
PROMOTIONS		ONLINE MARKETING		CONTINGENCY	
Sales promotions - consumer		Website development & maintenance	20,000	Contingency for unplanned items	39,000
Sales promotions – trade	20,000	Search engine advertising	10,000		
Sales incentive schemes	25,000	Search engine optimization (SEO)	2,000		
Trade shows & exhibitions	15,000	Database marketing	4,000		
Promotional videos & DVD's	10,000	Social media marketing	1,000		
Direct marketing	10,000				
Promotional merchandise	5,000				
SUB TOTAL	85,000	SUB TOTAL	37,000	TOTAL MARKETING BUDGET	$480,000

5.2 Marketing Financial Statement

The financial statement forecast shows sales of existing products will slow in the next three years but will be more than replaced by turnover generated from the launch of our new workstations products. We will spend considerably more than we have in the past on marketing to the extent that we are prepared to produce a marginal profit only in Year 1 in order to build profits in years 2 & 3 while maintaining a large investment in sales and marketing. The plan is based on achieving a net profit before tax of $615,000 in year 3 which will equate to 32% of gross turnover. We believe this forecast is achievable while recognizing that spend levels and investment in product innovation will need to be maintained in the development phase. The following profit and loss forecast is based on sales being achieved at the 'Most likely' level.

Marketing Financial Statement - Years 1 to 3

$000's	Year 1			Year 2			Year 3		
	Pessimistic	Most Likely	Optimistic	Pessimistic	Most Likely	Optimistic	Pessimistic	Most Likely	Optimistic
SALES									
Product 1 - Desks	630	700	770	570	630	690	510	560	625
Product 2 – Returns	180	200	220	160	180	200	145	160	180
Product 3 – Screens	90	100	110	80	90	100	73	85	90
Product 4 – Work stations	280	300	320	500	600	650	900	1095	1195
TOTAL REVENUE	1,180	1,300	1,420	1,310	1,500	1,640	1,628	1,900	2,090
Direct costs									
Product 1 - Desks	158	175	192	145	157	170	131	140	156
Product 2 - Returns	45	50	55	40	45	50	36	40	45
Product 3 - Screens	22	25	28	20	23	25	18	20	24
Product 4 – Work stations	70	75	80	125	150	165	225	275	300
TOTAL DIRECT COSTS	295	325	355	330	375	410	410	475	525
Gross margin	885	975	1,065	980	1,125	1,230	1,218	1,425	1,565
% of sales	75	75	75	75	75	75	75	75	75
LESS OPERATING COSTS									
Marketing	480	480	480	515	515	515	550	550	550
% of sales	41	37	34	39	34	31	34	29	26
Admin & overheads	240	240	240	250	250	250	260	260	260
% of sales	20	18	17	19	17	15	16	14	12
TOTAL OPERATING COSTS	720	720	720	765	765	765	810	810	810
% of sales	61	55	51	58	51	47	50	43	39
EARNING BEFORE INTEREST & TAX (EBIT)	165	255	345	215	360	465	408	615	755
% of sales	14	20	24	16	24	28	25	32	36

PART 6: IMPLEMENTATION & CONTROLS
6.1 Sales & marketing personnel

Mark will have responsibility for marketing and sales planning and implementation. He reports to Dennis who has overall responsibility for approval of plans and financial responsibility. Carol reports to Mark on receptionist/sales assistant and telesales responsibilities. Sally reports to Mark on marketing budget administration control. The sales representative appointee will report to Mark and share sales and customer service responsibilities.

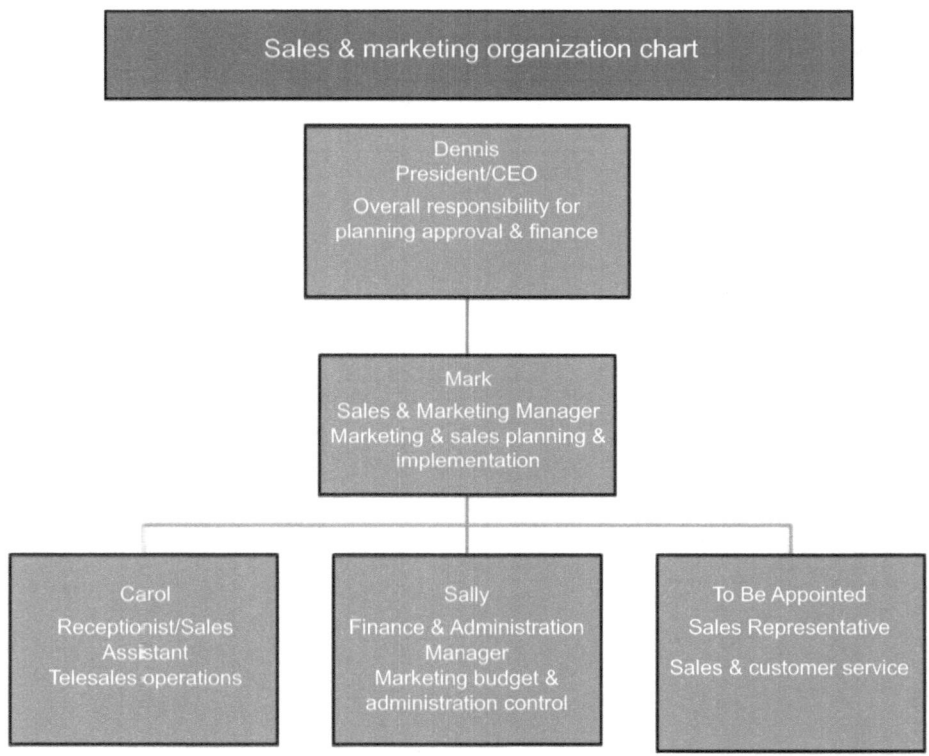

6.2 Action plan

The action plan for Stage 1 - the initial development stage is summarized below. This will subsequently be progressed to include Stage 2 – the commercial production and product launch stage and Stage 3 – post launch sales and marketing.

\	Action plan Stage 1. Pre-launch phase			
Development stage	Action steps	Target completion date	Person responsible	Results achieved
Market research	Qualitative consumer concept product research	Completed	Mark	Positive consumer demand confirmed. Improvements identified.
	Test reaction to prototype among target market	July 2017	Mark	Excellent responses received to date.
Product development	Research global development in work station modules	July 2017	Mark	Some good ideas identified from web research
	Finalize product design & specifications	September 2017	Mark/ Dennis	Preliminary designs look promising
	Product prototype	October 2017	Dennis	Produced on schedule
	Commence commercial production	January 2018	Dennis	On schedule
Packaging development	Commence flat pack design and specifications with packaging supplier	October 2017	Dennis/ Mark	On schedule
	Brief graphic designer for flat pack graphics design including essential text such as assembly instructions	October 2017	Mark	On schedule

6.3 Implementation schedule

The action plan will be synchronized to the following implementation schedule. Other components of the plan will be added as the launch roll-out progresses.

Implementation schedule

Plan Stage	Timing
Product development	May–Jun (Year 1)
Product design	Jun–Jul (Year 1)
Commercial factory production	Jul–Aug (Year 1)
Market research	Aug (Year 1)
Launch selling materials	Oct–Nov (Year 1)
Product sell-in	Jan–Feb (Year 2)
Distribution rollout	Apr–Jul (Year 2)
Advertising	Mar–Aug (Year 2)
Promotions	Mar; Aug–Nov (Year 2)
Merchandising	Jul–Nov (Year 2)
(Add other stages as required)	

Month: M J J A S O N D | J F M A M J J A S O N D
Year 1 | Year 2

6.4 Review & evaluation schedule

The schedule below will be progressively developed as the launch program rolls out. Monitoring and evaluation of results achieved will provide the opportunity for timely and effective remedial action.

Review and evaluation schedule

Plan Stage	Progress Evaluation	Effectiveness (1 – 10)	Proposed Changes	For action by
Product development	Outstanding concept developed	9	Modifications required to locking device	Dennis
Product design completion	Designs completed on time and on budget	8	Modifications to desking screens required	Dennis
Commercial Production	Excellent quality. Need more flexibility to meet immediate orders	8	We need some adjustments to factory stock levels	Dennis
Market Research	Need more info on price elasticity	8	Implement a study among initial purchasers to include price reaction	Mark
Launch materials	On time and on budget. Worked well	9	No further action required	N/A
Product sell in	On schedule. Could have done better detailing concept to retail sales people	7	Need to start planning for expansion into other markets	Mark
Distribution	Mostly on schedule. Missed a couple of important deadlines	6	Need to review further stockists opportunities	Mark
Advertising	Seems to be working well. Retailers like it.	8	More of the same for now	Mark
Promotions	Budget for temporary price reductions overspent but concept worked well	6	Need tighter controls to monitor allowances for temporary price reductions	Mark
Merchandising	Only 65% of targeted in-store displays achieved in first year	6	Consider engaging a part time merchandiser to assemble and erect displays in accordance with agreements reached with store managers.	Mark

GLOSSARY

Above-the-line refers to all expenditure on media advertising such as in newspapers, magazines, TV, radio, outdoor or transportation. More recently internet advertising in all its forms has been added to this category. (See also 'Below-the-line')

Advertising The use of paid media by a seller to communicate persuasive information about its goods or services.

AdWords: A targeted advertising program in which business ads appear as "sponsored links" on the Google results pages. The advertiser chooses keywords and a short one or two line text ad, which is displayed on the results pages when the ad keywords match up with the search keywords. The order of ads is determined by several factors. One is the amount advertisers are willing to pay Google for a user to click their ad, and others are the relevance of the ad to the search and the historical click-through rate of the ad. The overall quality score also influences an ad's position on the Google network, as well as affecting the calculation of a keyword's minimum bid.

Affiliate marketing: a method of promoting web businesses in which an affiliate is rewarded for every visitor, subscriber and/or customer provided through their efforts. It is similar to the established concept of being paid a finder's fee for the introduction of new clients to a business.

Below-the-line refers to all other promotional activities apart from media advertising such as price oriented offers, point-of-sale advertising, competitions and contests, merchandising, publicity, personal selling, direct marketing, eCommerce and many more.

B2B: (Businesses to Businesses). Businesses involved in marketing products or services to other businesses.

B2C. (Businesses to consumers). Businesses involved in marketing products or services to consumers.

Blogs: The word blog is derived from 'web' and 'log'. It is a form of online journal or web site that allows you to write about your subject or field and obtain feedback from readers. Blogs are often posted to popular blog platforms such as WordPress and BlogSpot. Blogging can be a highly effective marketing strategy particularly when targeting Gen Y or Z.

Brand equity: The ability the brand has accrued over time to command higher sales and profits compared with generic and competitive brands.

Brand Extension: The process of using an established brand name for an addition to the product range.

Brand Image is the sum of associations, characteristics and attributes that exist in audience's minds about the brand. e.g. A leader in technology, innovative, premium quality, etc.

Brand personality assigns human characteristics to a brand. e.g. warm, likeable, friendly, approachable, etc.

Consignment stock is stock owned by one party, but held and not paid for by another until sold.

Consumer durables are long life products such as cars and household appliances such as refrigerators, washing machines and dishwashers, etc. Because of the relatively high unit costs of these products, they are carefully considered purchases.

Content marketing is any marketing format that involves the creation and sharing of media and publishing content in order to acquire customers. It can include text, blogs, eBooks, press releases, tweets, video, audio and online events. It is a marketing technique of creating and distributing valuable, relevant and consistent content across multiple channels and devices to attract and acquire a clearly defined audience – with the objective of driving profitable customer action.

Customer Relationship Management (CRM) A term that refers to practices, strategies and technologies that companies use to manage and analyze customer interactions and data throughout the customer life cycle, with the goal of improving business relationships with customers, assisting in customer retention and driving sales growth.

Customer engagement is the depth of the relationship a customer has with a company or brand.

Customer service. The act of taking care of the customer's needs by providing and delivering professional, helpful, high quality service and assistance before, during, and after the customer's requirements are met.

Cut through The ability of an advertisement or advertising campaign with enough impact to 'cut through' the advertising clutter that bombards our daily lives.

Database marketing is an evolutionary refinement of direct marketing using computer databases that are continually updated with customers and prospects records such as buying history, demographics, personal preferences and so forth.

Direct Marketing is a branch of marketing that communicates directly to target markets via 'addressable media' such as mail, telemarketing and email.

Early adopter is an individual or business who uses a new product or technology before others.

EBIT: Earnings before interest and tax.

eCommerce: Business transactions conducted over the Internet

Fast moving consumer goods (FMCG) also known as Consumer Packaged Goods are products that are used on an everyday basis, that are not carefully considered purchases. They are high turnover relatively low margin products.

Focus groups is a form of qualitative market research in which trained moderators lead a series of group discussions of up to 12 respondents representative of the target market.

Generations X, Y & Z. It can be beneficial to use 'Generation' definitions in defining target market demographics such as 'Baby Boomers' born between 1946 to 1964, Generation 'X' born between 1965 to 1977, Generation 'Y' (or Millennials) born between 1978 to 1994 and Generation 'Z' born since 1995.

Google Analytics A free platform that allows you to measure and analyze your website traffic.

Gross profit: Sales value less all costs directly related to those sales. These costs can include manufacturing expenses, raw materials, labor, sales, marketing, distribution and other expenses.

Gross Margin is a required income statement entry that reflects total revenue minus cost of goods sold (COGS). Gross margin is a company's profit before operating expenses, interest payments and taxes. Gross margin is also known as gross profit.

Horizontal integration: The term refers to a company's seeking ownership or increased control of some of its competitors. (See also vertical integration).

Impulse sales: Sales that were not planned or premeditated by customers.

Inbound marketing is about providing relevant and informative material when prospects come looking for your products or services. Such activities include blogs, podcasts, newsletters E-zines, newsletters, eBooks, webinars, etc. (See also 'Outbound marketing').

Inorganic growth: The process of growing a business through mergers, takeovers and acquisitions. (See also organic growth.)

Key Performance Indicators (KPI's) Measurements that quantify marketing or other business performance achievements such as market share and response rates from advertising, database marketing, sales calls, etc. KPI's are also sometimes referred to as Marketing Metrics.

Line extension: The process of increasing the company's product range.

List price is the price stated in a price list or catalogue and is often the starting point and is subject to discounts.

Logo (Logotype) A distinctive stylized company signature, trademark, brand name, typeface or slogan.

Market segmentation: The process of dividing a market into distinct and meaningful groups of buyers who might merit separate products and/or marketing mixes. For example, the furniture market may be divided into two main market segments: commercial and domestic.

Market sub-segments: A further division of a market segment. For example, the commercial furniture market segment can be divided into office, hospitality, entertainment, retail, medical and educational.

Market The set of all actual and potential buyers of a product or service.

Marketer: A marketing practitioner such as marketing, product and brand managers.

Market leader: A brand, product, or firm that has the largest percentage of total sales revenue (the market share) of a market. A market leader often dominates its competitors in customer loyalty, distribution coverage, image, perceived value, price, profit, and promotional spending.

Marketing audit: the systematic collection, analysis and evaluation of information relating to the internal and external environments that determine the situation the company or organization currently occupies.

Marketing metrics Refers to any aspect of marketing that can be measured and quantified such as sales, brand awareness, market share, return on marketing investment, customer retention rate and response rates from advertising, database marketing, sales calls, etc. Also referred to as Key Performance Indicators or KPI's.

Marketing mix: The particular blend of controllable marketing variables that the firm uses to achieve its objectives in the target market. Often referred to as the 4P's – Product, Place, Price and Promotion.

Market research: The process of determining the size, shape and trends in a market overall. e.g. the market for office furniture. (See also 'marketing research').

Marketing research: The systematic design, collection, analysis and reporting of data and findings relevant to a specific marketing decision making process.

Marketing strategy and marketing tactics: Marketing strategy is a broad statement relating to how you are going to meet a goal or objective e.g. we will use email marketing to communicate with existing customers. Marketing tactics are more precise actions that are designed to implement a broader strategy e.g. we will collect customer's email addresses from on-line product registrations.

Mass marketing: A style of marketing in which the seller mass produces and mass distributes one product and attempts to attract everyone to its purchase.

Merchandising Refers to the variety of products available at retail level and the display of those products in such a way that it stimulates interest and entices customers to make a purchase.

Millennials. A person reaching young adulthood around the year 2000. (Also known as 'Generation Y')

Mission statement: This is an expression of the business's reason for existence, what it wants to accomplish and be recognized for. The mission statement should include community and employee values and benefits and not just plain commercial goals. It states what your company "stands for" in the marketplace.

Net profit: Often referred to as the bottom line, calculated by subtracting a company's total expenses from total revenue, showing what the company has earned (or lost) in a given period (usually one year).

GLOSSARY

Organic growth: The process of growing a business through increased sales from within the business. (See also inorganic growth).

Outbound marketing is about sending your marketing message to as many people as possible through traditional forms of mass media such as TV, radio, billboards, print ads etc. (See also 'inbound marketing").

Pay-per-click (PPC), also known as cost per click (CPC), is an internet advertising model used to direct traffic to websites, in which an advertiser pays a publisher (typically a search engine or website owner) when the ad is clicked.

Plan-o-grams set out recommended shelf layouts for the entire product category including competitors' products. They can ensure that a company's products receive at least proportionate shelf space to market share (but preferably more).

Podcast: A digital audio file made available on the Internet for downloading to a computer or portable media player, typically available as a series, new instalments of which can be received by subscribers automatically. It usually has a format similar to a radio or television show.

Primary research: The process of finding specific information that is not already available from existing sources. It requires the commissioning of special quantitative or qualitative research studies.

Prime prospects: The main group in a target market that offers the largest sales potential.

Product positioning: Product positioning is concerned with creating a distinctive niche in the consumers mind. It is how you want your product to be perceived. It's what differentiates your product from competitors. Positioning can be based on projected users, usage occasions, lifestyle implications, price points or quality attributes.

Product proposition: The benefit that is offered to the target market that is intrinsic to the product.

Product segment: A sub-sector of a larger product category e.g. the office furniture market may be segmented into seating, storage systems, built-in furniture and freestanding furniture.

Promotion is the process of communicating with the target market in order to persuade them to purchase your products or services.

Pull strategy: A strategy that calls for high investment in advertising and promotions aimed at the final consumer to build up demand for the product.

Push strategy: A strategy that calls for using the sales force and trade promotion to push the product through the channels of distribution.

Qualitative research: Research that gathers attitudes and opinions representative of the target group as a whole.

Quantitative research is research such as consumer surveys that are statistically valid and can be measured numerically and where findings can be statistically analyzed.

Reach and frequency: Reach refers to the number of persons in the target market (expressed as a percentage) who are exposed to the advertising message in a given media schedule while the frequency is the average number of times the target market sees or hears the message. Target Audience Rating Points (TARPS) are calculated by multiplying reach by frequency.

Respondents: Subjects of marketing research surveys who are representative of the target market for the product or service being researched.

Retail markup: A percentage added to the cost to get to the retail selling price.

Sales funnel: The buying process that companies lead customers through when purchasing products. A sales funnel is divided into several steps, which differ according to the particular sales model in question. A typical sales funnel would have the following steps in a chain: Awareness (of your products or services) > Leads generated > Prospects > Customers.

Sales promotion is the term used to describe all the activities you devise to increase sales apart from media advertising. The main objective of sales promotion is to provide consumers with an additional reason to purchase and to stimulate product trial. More tactical in nature than strategic.

Sales revenue is the money an enterprise generates in the sale of its goods or services. Also referred as 'turnover'.

Secondary research: The process of gathering information that already exists from existing internal sources (such as sales records) or external sources (such as government industry reports, etc.)

Search Engine Optimization (SEO): The technical steps that need to be taken to make your site 'Search Engine Friendly'. This involves code, design and layout.

Search Engine Advertising (SEA): Involves Pay per Click (PPC) advertising (such as Google AdWords) aimed at getting your site in the top sponsored links positions on search results pages.

SME's: Small to Medium Enterprises. The sizes vary from country to country and according to who is giving the definition. For the purposes of this guide, small businesses are defined as those with less than ten full time employees while medium enterprises are defined as those with less than 100 employees.

Social media essentially is a category of online platforms in which people are talking, participating, sharing, networking, and bookmarking online. There is a wide variety of social media, ranging from social sharing sites such as YouTube, Vimeo and Flickr through social networks such as LinkedIn, Instagram, Snapchat, Twitter and Facebook.

Social media advertising: Advertising in social media platforms (such as Facebook, YouTube etc.). Can be accurately targeted against very specific target markets. Rapidly growing at the expense of traditional media.

Sponsorship is providing financial support in cash or kind for an event, activity, person or organization or through the provision of products or services in return for naming rights and other benefits.

Strategic planning: The managerial process of developing and maintaining a strategic fit between the organization and its changing market opportunities. It relies on developing a clear company mission, objectives and goals, growth strategies and product portfolios.

Sweepstakes Promotional schemes in which prizes are given to winners selected only by chance from the entries received. Sweepstakes do not require a purchase consideration. Otherwise they would become a lottery (which often requires a licence to operate).

Target audience: The demographic or lifestyle group that advertising is intended to reach.

Target market: A well-defined set of customers whose needs the company plans to satisfy.

Target marketing: The process of selecting one or more of the defined market segments and developing a positioning and marketing strategy for each.

TARPS: An acronym for Target Audience Rating Points - a term used in audience research to measure the audience a commercial reaches. If a TV or radio commercial is seen by 10 percent of the target audience it achieves 10 rating points. When all the TARPS are aggregated over the course of a campaign, they become Gross Rating Points (GRP's).

Test market is a tightly controlled test that uses real-life scenarios and consumers to evaluate a product's potential in a small scale geographical sample that is representative of the total population.

Trademark: A brand or part of a brand that has legal protection because it is capable of exclusive appropriation. A trademark protects the seller's exclusive rights to use the brand name and /or brand mark.

Umbrella branding: The practice of marketing several products from one company under a single brand name instead of a series of different 'personality' brands for each product range.

Unique selling proposition (USP): An offer, which has specific benefits to the user, and which the competition cannot or does not offer. It is so strong that it will attract new customers to your product or service.

URL Short for universal resource locator includes the protocol (ex. HTTP, FTP), the domain name (or IP address), and additional path information (folder/file). On the Web, a URL may address a web page file, image file, or any other file supported by the HTTP protocol.

Vertical integration: The process in which several steps in the production and/or distribution of a product or service are controlled by a single company, in order to increase that company's size in the marketplace.

Viral Marketing: Also known as "word-of-mouth" recommendation passed on from one consumer to another person to person, or using websites, email or social networks such as Facebook, and YouTube. Viral Marketing is a potent (and cost effective) marketing strategy because personal recommendation is more credible than paid media.

Wear out: The point reached when an advertising campaign loses its effectiveness due to repeat overplay of advertisements or commercials. Wear out with the consumer is often reached long after the point it is reached with the advertiser who is constantly exposed to it.

YouTube is a video sharing service where users can create their own profile, upload videos, watch, like and comment on other videos. It can be a valuable tool in social media marketing.

— THE NEXT STEPS —

Having got to this point you are well on your way to developing a dynamic marketing plan tailored to meet the needs of your individual business.

You will have gained an appreciation of the content you should consider in your plan and the structure needed to develop a series of coordinated strategies that will take your business to the next more profitable stage of development.

To download the free Microsoft Word document *Marketing Plan Builder templates* go to www.marketingplanbuilder.com, then scroll down to the link at the foot of the home page. When downloaded go to View >Edit.

Then begin the process of building your plan with the templates provided. At each step there are pointers, to remind you of the content applicable to that step as well as reference keys to help you determine which templates are relevant to your business class and the plan level you wish to complete.

It is recommended that you copy and paste the individual templates that you select for your plan into a clean Microsoft Word document with a separate page for each template. This will avoid possible formatting and layout issues.

When you have completed the selected templates in the clean document, with any commentary you deem relevant to add, you can format the completed plan to your personal preferences.

It is suggested that you develop your plan in manageable 'bite sized chunks'. Complete the templates to the basic stage initially, then go on to the more intermediate or advanced stages as your knowledge base of the planning process grows and as your understanding of the market in which you are competing increases.

Try to get into the habit of allocating an hour a day to developing the plan. You will be rewarded by realizing how much your understanding of the market and the business you are in grow as you progress through the planning process.

When the plan is completed you will be ready to start its implementation that will lead you to giving your business the focus and direction to reach its full potential.

The publishers of *Marketing Plan Builder* wish you the satisfaction to be gained from attaining this achievement.

One last thought dear readers. We sincerely hope you have found this book to be a useful reference guide to the growth of your business. If you give it the 'thumbs up', it would be greatly appreciated if you would pen a brief review of the book in the Amazon Kindle product detail page. And if you have any comments or suggestions as to how we could improve this book in the next edition, we would be pleased to get your feedback at: *info@kestermarketing.com.au*

ABOUT THE AUTHOR

Garth Kester has pursued a lifelong career in marketing in a variety of senior executive and consulting roles in Australia and internationally. His depth of experience has included account service and strategic planning positions with leading international advertising agencies and marketing management roles in national and multinational consumer goods companies. These positions took him to the UK, USA, South Africa and Europe where he contributed to worldwide marketing projects.

Following corporate roles he has operated a proprietary marketing consultancy in which he has undertaken countless assignments for a diverse range of business models from fast moving consumer goods and consumer durables to transport services, leisure, real estate and textiles industries. Enterprise sizes have covered the spectrum from micro-businesses through to large conglomerates.

This broad marketing background has yielded unique 'real world' insights into what makes marketing strategies effective at a practical "hands on" level. It has also provided an ability to accurately assess and distil clients' needs into actionable plans that achieve rewarding outcomes.

He is a noted keynote speaker in his area of expertise and is well known for his work in corporate communications and industry analysis.

This broad body of practical experience is encapsulated in the many insights assembled in this book.

Index

A

About the author 183
Above the line 45, 71.
    See also Below the line
Advertising 79
  Media selection 85
  Setting objectives 80
  Responsibility allocation 81
  Setting the budget 82, 83
Advertising agencies 11
Advertising Research 88
AdWords 94
Affiliate marketing 176
Anecdotal evidence 29, 31

B

B2B (See also B2C) 2
B2C (See also B2B) 2
Baby Boomers 37, 177
Below the line 45, 56.
    See also Above the line
Blogs 14
Boston Consulting Group Matrix 20
Brand equity 54
Brand extension 176
Brand Image 56
Branding 54
Brand personality 56
Business Location 64

C

Competitor Analysis 26
Consignment stock 68
Consumer durables 53, 176
Content marketing 94
Corporate communications 106
Corporate Image 57
Critical issues 40
CRM (Customer Relationship Management) 74
Customer engagement 177
Customer focus 6, 7, 77
Customer Relations 78
Customer Service 76
Cut through 177

D

Database Marketing 66, 108, 169, 177.
See also Direct marketing
David Ogilvy 55, 84
Demographics 37
Direct marketing 108, 110, 169, 177.
See also Database marketing
Distribution 66
Distribution Channel Partners Business Maximization 68
Drucker, Peter 14

E

Early adopters 134
eCommerce 39, 66, 94
Emery, Albert 7
Executive summary 16
Sales Development Techniques 74

F

Facebook 180
Financial statements 112
   Marketing budget 112
   Marketing Financial Statement 114
Flickr 180
FMCG 45
Focus groups 11
Four Ps of marketing, The 47

G

Generations X Y & Z 37, 177
Google analytics 94
Gross margin 147
Gross profit 18

H

Horizontal integration 177.
See also Vertical integration
How to use marketing plan builder 4

I

Implementation and controls 116
   Action plan 117
   Implementation schedule 118
   Review and evaluation schedule 120
   Sales and marketing personnel resources 116
Impulse sales 100
Inbound marketing 14, 177.
See also Outbound marketing
Inorganic growth 177.
See also Organic growth

Instagram 180

K

KPI's (Key Performance Indicators) 12

L

Line extension 178
LinkedIn 180
List price 147
Logo (logotype) 143
Lord Leverhulme 81

M

Mahatma Gandhi 78
Marketers 6
Marketing audit 178
Marketing definitions 6
Marketing explained 6
Marketing Financial Statements
   Financial statements 114
   Marketing budget 112
Marketing metrics 178
Marketing mix 47
Marketing myopia 7
Marketing objectives 42
Marketing plan elements 15
Marketing plans, business plans and strategic plans 9
Marketing research 7, 10, 29.
See also Market research
Marketing strategy 45.
See also Marketing tactics 178
Market leader 43

Market research 6, 7, 10.
See also Marketing research
Market research firms 29
Market segmentation 22
Market sub-segments 178
Mass marketing 178
Media selection 79, 80, 85
Merchandising 100
Micro businesses 71
Millennials 37
Mission statements 35

N

Net profit 17

O

On-line marketing and eCommerce 93
Organic growth 179.
See also Inorganic growth
Outbound marketing 14, 179.
See also Inbound marketing

P

Packaging 58
Pay per Click 179, 180
Place 64
Plan-o-grams 101
Podcasts 98
Positioning 51
Price 59
Price Brands 55
Price sensitivity 60
Price Strategies 61

Price Tactics 63
Primary research 10, 29, 179.
See also Secondary research
Prime prospects 23
Product life cycles 13
Product (or Service) Segmentation 23
Product propositions 53
Product Segmentation by Channels of Distribution 25
Products or Services Review 21
Promotion 71
Psychographics 37
Public relations and publicity 102
Pull strategy 179. *See also* Push strategy
Push strategy 179. *See also* Pull strategy

Q

Qualitative research 11, 29, 179.
See also Quantitative research
Quantitative research 11, 29, 179.
See also Qualitative research

R

Reach and frequency 82
Respondents 179
Retail markup 180
Rosser Reeves 49

S

Sales Analysis 18
Sales Development 73
Sales development techniques
    Existing customers 74

New customers 75

Sales Force Management 71

Sales Funnel 73

Sales & market review 17

Sales Promotion 89

Sales revenue 180

Sample marketing plan 123

Search Engine Advertising (SEA) 97

Search Engine Optimization (SEO) 96

Secondary research 10, 180.

See also Primary research

SME's (Small to Medium Enterprises) 2

Snapchat 180

Social media advertising 85

Social media marketing 98

Sponsorship 105

Strategic planning 180

Supply Chain Management 69

Sweepstakes 89

SWOT Analysis 32

T

Target audience 85

Target markets 37

TARPS (Target Audience Rating Points) 82

Test markets 29

The military analogy 7

The new paradigm in marketing 14

The next steps 182

Theodore Levitt 7

Trademark 181

Trade shows and exhibitions 92

Twitter 180

U

Umbrella branding 181

URL (Universal Resource Locator) 96

USP (Unique Selling Proposition) 49

V

Vertical integration 181.

See also Horizontal integration

Viral marketing 14

W

Wear out 181

Website functionality 94

Website promotion strategies 96

What can a marketing plan do for your business? 8

Y

YouTube 180, 181.

NOTES

www.ingramcontent.com/pod-product-compliance
Lightning Source LLC
Chambersburg PA
CBHW020652220526
45464CB00001B/406